# OVER HERE

# OVER HERE
## *Criticizing America, 1968–1989*

*Thomas R. Edwards*

RUTGERS UNIVERSITY PRESS
*New Brunswick, New Jersey*

Library of Congress Cataloging-in-Publication Data

Edwards, Thomas R., 1928–
  Over here : criticizing America, 1968–1989 / Thomas R. Edwards.
    p.   cm.
  ISBN 0-8135-1709-5 (cloth)—ISBN 0-8135-1710-9 (pbk.)
  1. United States—Civilization—1970–   2. Literature,
American—20th century—Social aspects.   3. Authors, American—20th
century—Political and social views.   I. Title.
E169.12.E35   1991
973.92—dc20                                                          91-14058
                                                                                                    CIP

British Cataloging-in-Publication information available

Copyright © 1991 by Thomas R. Edwards
All rights reserved
Manufactured in the United States of America

*For Richard Poirier*

# Contents

Preface / ix
Acknowledgments / xiii

CRY WOLFE •
McLuhan's Medium / 1
The New West / 17
No Country for Old Men / 25
Radical Chic / 39

• • •

Thinking about Sports / 45
Manson Country / 55
Women's Fiction / 67
Tough Guys / 81

THE RED MENACE •
Politics and Feeling / 91
The Nixoniad / 99

ENEMIES •
Terror in Freedonia / 107
The Power of Art / 117

• • •

Stage and Screen / 125
Updike's Rabbit / 137

| | |
|---|---|
| DEMOCRATIC VISTAS • | *Good Morning, America* / 149 |
| | *Crackpot Crusoe* / 163 |
| A SENSE OF THE PAST • | *The American Exemption* / 171 |
| | *After the Fall* / 181 |
| | *The Dark Side* / 193 |
| AMERICAN POPS • | *Gulp!* / 201 |
| | *The Real World* / 209 |

. . .

*Small Expectations* / 221
*Macho Man* / 231

*Index* / 241

# *Preface*

> The ear loves names of foreign and classical topography. But here we are; and, if we will tarry a little, we may come to learn that here is best. See to it, only, that thyself is here.
> —*Emerson, "Heroism" (1841)*

These commentaries, written over two decades, have to do with American writing, and less directly with America itself, in troubled times. Between the later 1960s and the later 1980s, as some of us remember well enough, many received ideas about America's values and its destiny were severely tried, and some of them were convicted of arrogance, folly, or impossibility in a new historical situation. Though I wrote these pieces separately and with no conscious program in mind, they now seem to me dimly to reflect my own efforts to acknowledge various failures of our national expectations even while continuing to suppose that for someone like me, in Emerson's words, "here is best" after all.

Though the tone is often personal, I was not trying to write about myself. But conscientious criticism describes acts of reading which in some way involve, or threaten, the critic, and the reader may wish to know just who I think I am. I am

American-born (on Columbus Day, by a happy chance), a white, Anglo-Saxon, (lapsed) Protestant male, a middle-aged, middle-class husband and father. My politics are not very cogent, mixing old-style liberal concern for the general welfare with an old-style conservative suspicion that new is not always better and that you should spend only what you have. (I don't often recognize much of myself in persons who now call themselves liberals or conservatives.) Born in the Middle West, I was brought up and educated in the Northeast, and since then I have taught literature, though not American literature, on both coasts. If I'm an academic intellectual of some sort, I'm also an amateur businessman with interests in the Deep South. As an identity, this one, with all its middles and straddles, makes very little sense, in itself a familiar American plight.

Yet such incoherence may at least aid observation, since the observer carries so little programmatic luggage with him to the viewing point. Rereading these pieces, I heard myself hoping to find that the writers I was discussing knew something about American experience that sounded right to me, or, much better, that they knew things I didn't know but could learn to accept as authentic and important. Considerations of genre or cultural level were thus secondary; there are comments here on fiction, on journalistic writing, on literary and cultural criticism, on both "serious" and "popular" arts, and I was usually less anxious to categorize than to weigh whatever the writers were doing against my own sense of the realities they meant to evoke.

The risk in speaking so casually of "realities" is of course immense. The America I think I know is obviously no more real than anyone else's, and I was, after all, reporting about books, writing, language, and not about my own unmediated encounters with events. Some literary theorists now warn against referring writing to life at all, for what are good, if not, for me, quite sufficient reasons. But what anyone knows about America is already largely linguistic. It cannot readily

*Preface* xi

be detached from the words, idioms, rhythms, tones, and accents of American speech, whether heard in the street or in the language of those literary masters—Emerson, Whitman, Twain, Hemingway, Faulkner, Frost, and Williams among them—who tried to "write in American" about what they knew. Admittedly there is no one American voice, in life or books, nor any representation of such a voice that is wholly untouched by outside sources and models. What we speak is "English," and what we say in it is colored by social, regional, and ethnic habits whose roots may grow much farther away than England, just as even the most defiantly "Amur'k'n" literary style, as Pound approvingly called Frost's, betrays some consciousness of how writers elsewhere have or might have put it. (The irony in the title "Over Here" is deliberate.) But Americans have a shrewd and suspicious ear for the foreign and the affected, and recognizing America in writing includes hearing the written words as some conceivable version of American speech.

The matter of language is, however, usually not a primary theme in these writings, which I chose for inclusion largely because they deal with books in which contemporary American events and concerns are the subject or an aspect of the method—politics, war, the economy, the media, private or public crime, popular styles that say something about our character and mood. I should add that they were not chosen for the merely literary importance of their subjects; I've omitted pieces on American writers whom I value more *as* writers than many of those discussed here—such as John Barth, Thomas Berger, Don de Lillo, Stanley Elkin, Joseph Heller, Norman Mailer, Toni Morrison, Joyce Carol Oates, Ishmael Reed, and Philip Roth—either because my comments on them didn't closely enough engage the "American" theme or because what I wrote about them now seems too brief or unremarkable to be worth repeating.

Whatever the subjects or occasions, I hope that this book

shows how my pleasure in being over here has complicated my frequent dismay about what America has been like during these years. (To smuggle in some foreign wisdom, from Jane Austen, "one does not love a place the less for having suffered in it.") I see that there may be a certain nostalgia in my enterprise, a turning toward home after mental absence or neglect. But it is not chauvinism or boosterism, some reductive Literary Americanism, that is being advanced here. It would be silly to argue that good writing needs to be "American" in my present sense, and writing that is so may often be no good. I've merely tried to understand certain accounts of recent American experience *as* an American reader, a participant—if not always a joyful one—in the general life they refer to, and not as a reader safely distanced from that life by some presumed advantage of cosmopolitan taste and cultural privilege. Mindful of Emerson's warning, I try to see to it that myself is here.

I've made some small corrections for the benefit of grammar, clarity, and sense, and restored a few flourishes that editors talked me out of, but otherwise the pieces stand as they first appeared, except that some have been detached from what were longer articles and a number have been retitled. Rather than grouping them topically, I preferred to follow the order of their writing, making a kind of unshaped chronicle that may keep some of the feel of living through a period in which clear ideas of significance and continuity were hard to come by, moment by moment. Not everyone who endured these years will have felt about them just as I did; but I do hope to provoke some to be moved and instructed by their memories of their own responses, however different. And of course I hope to suggest to younger readers something of what a strange and exciting time it was.

# *Acknowledgments*

If only to prove that no good deed goes unpunished, I wish I could mention by name the people, both friends and strangers, who bothered to say that they liked some of these writings or others of the same sort; fortunately for them, perhaps, they are too numerous to be so acknowledged, but I do remember their kindness. I'm grateful to the various editors who found things for me to write about and let me imagine that the results were adequate. I thank Kenneth Arnold, Leslie Mitchner, and Stuart Mitchner, of Rutgers University Press, for making things easier than I had expected; also Suzanne Hyman and everyone else at *Raritan*, for being so nice to work with. And Nancy, Sarah, and John Edwards helped by trying to keep me up to date, and by taking me (at most) no more seriously than I deserved.

The dedication is to someone whose example, for a very long time now, has kept me mindful of what careful reading involves, and why it matters.

These essays were first published in: *The New York Review of Books* ("Tough Guys," "Terror in Freedonia," "Stage and Screen," "Good Morning, America," "The American Exemption," "The Dark Side," "Gulp!" "The Real World," "Small

Expectations," "Macho Man"); *Partisan Review* ("McLuhan's Medium," "The New West," "No Country for Old Men," "Thinking about Sports," "Manson Country," "Women's Fiction"); *The New York Times Book Review* ("Radical Chic," "Politics and Feeling," "The Nixoniad," "Crackpot Crusoe"); *The New Republic* ("The Power of Art"); *The Atlantic* ("Updike's Rabbit"); *Raritan: A Quarterly Review* ("After the Fall").

# OVER HERE

*I begin somewhere north of the border, but what we down here so presumptuously like to call "America" is very much at issue in my reading of Marshall McLuhan. In 1968 I thought he was being taken much too seriously, both by those who embraced his ideas about media and by those who indignantly rejected them as threatening the imminent death of literacy and reason. I don't suppose that his work seems nearly so exciting or dangerous now (but see "After the Fall"), and this familiarity may have its cost; as I tried to suggest, he did know something important about how information affects us, and my remarks meant to sound affectionate and not wholly disrespectful.*

# *McLuhan's Medium*
(1968)

Though it's hard to believe that many people really read or talk much about Marshall McLuhan these days, he and his critics keep electing him man of the decade. Frank Kermode remarked in 1963 that "in a truly literate society [*The Gutenberg Galaxy*] would start a long debate," but no one has waited for so improbable a millennium; McLuhan goes on writing new books and republishing old ones, but it hardly matters, since the debate about him now seems to have become self-generating. In *McLuhan: Hot & Cool,* an intriguing new olio of things by and about the master, we are assured of his importance by ad men, hip Jesuits, Susan Sontag, and various Canadians, assured of his folly by Dwight Macdonald, George P. Elliott, Christopher Ricks, and other Urizenic tyrants of typographical law, assured of his mixed value by judicious Centrists like Harold Rosenberg, Jonathan Miller, and George Steiner. But no one, least of all McLuhan himself, doubts that he has to be dealt with somehow. What is his fatal fascination? How can a mind that is by any known test slipshod and derivative, a style that so relentlessly cultivates the tasteless and the banal, occupy so much critical space? How can someone who solemnly assures us that "the word parody means a road that goes alongside another road" be trusted with any harder science than Greek etymologies?

I think it best to assume that *what* McLuhan says is the

least important thing about him. McLuhanism is not a message but a medium, a rendering of the uneasy excitement about contemporary culture that grips thoughtful people of a certain age. To my knowledge none of the contributors to *Hot & Cool* is under thirty, and for the people who are creating the new state of things or will have to live longest with it, McLuhan himself is nearly irrelevant. The lumpen-youth, in whom his prognostics seem best realized, don't read much and don't need him to tell them where they are, while their more clerkly peers, still provisionally interested in print and rational operations, find him superficial and old hat. For them the electronic culture is also a paperback culture, and they read or at least carry Lévi-Strauss and Fanon, not *Understanding Media*. McLuhan's audience consists mostly of people like himself and me, serious, adult, bookish souls formed by the literary culture of the twenties and thirties but anxious to feel up to date and touchingly sure that an intelligent reader of Joyce and Eliot can grasp just about anything if he puts his mind to it. There are no essays in *Hot & Cool* by psychologists or communications scientists—the wise, apparently, are saying nothing till they see.

McLuhan is *our* sage, alas. Like us, he can apprehend technical innovation only through analogy. Like us, he can do "research" only by pasting up other people's discoveries. Like us, he wants badly to have a sense of humor, keep cool and witty in the face of seeming nightmare, respond openly to the new without quite yielding to its seductions, remain critically objective without holing up in pedantry and moral fogeyism. His task has been to find a style, an expressive medium for his predicament and ours, and it's his style, in the largest sense, that here concerns me.

He seems most at home in the give-and-take of interview and conversation, where his method of "probing"—saying anything that seems provocative, regardless of contextual relevance or rational substance—works more freely than it can in premeditated print. The most revealing piece in *Hot & Cool* is a transcript of conversations with G. E. Stearn, from which I detach a representative and topical moment:

> STEARN: Similarly, you claim that the war in Vietnam is, more or less, a creature of television.
>
> MCLUHAN: Without an informed public there would be no war. We live in an informational environment and war is conducted with information. TV news coverage of Vietnam has been a disaster as far as Washington is concerned because it has alienated people altogether from that war. Newspaper coverage would never alienate people from the war because it's "hot," it doesn't involve. TV does and creates absolute nausea. It's like public hangings—if there were public hangings there would be no hangings. Because public hangings would *involve* people. The distant statistical fact—"At 5:30 this morning so and so was executed"—that's hot. Washington is still fighting a "hot" war, as it were, by newspaper means and the old technologies. The effects of the new technologies on war coverage is not something Washington is prepared to cope with. In Washington people do not concede that the news on TV and news in the press are dissimilar.
>
> TV has begun to dissolve the fabric of American life. All the assumptions—all the ground rules—based on visuality, superficiality, blueprinting, connectedness, equality, sameness—disappear with TV.
>
> STEARN: If you shut off TV, then we would end the war in Vietnam and at the same time set back the civil rights movement?
>
> MCLUHAN: Oh yes. But there is an alternative: Put hundreds of extra lines on the TV image, step up its

> visual intensity to a new hot level. This might serve to reverse the whole effect of TV. It might make the TV image photographic, slick, like movies: hot and detached. . . .

Now it isn't one's conditioning by print culture that creates this air of affable nuttiness. You could print these remarks, hear them sung by the Fugs, watch them dance in a TV cartoon or flash across the Astrodome scoreboard, and they still would conjure up the dense cross-purposes of Absurdist comedy. It plays into McLuhan's hand to get angry about such talk, but its dramatistic qualities are worth examining.

Here the character named "McLuhan" (clearly the star part) has a number of voices and roles at his disposal. He can be numbingly platitudinous ("TV has begun to dissolve the fabric of American life"), vocally just a halftone from the Sunday-supplement moralizer's determination to rescue us from life as it is. But this voice has a way of going a little askew, as a surprise term galvanizes the cliché with a twitch of pseudo-life—"without an informed public there would be no *war*" is like an unexpected gift you don't quite know how to accept. Another voice delights in the offhand analogy that proves exactly what it doesn't want to, like the remark about hangings. Public hangings did indeed "involve people," but as the testimony of eighteenth-century observers like Boswell makes clear, those people—the avid spectators and the pitifully histrionic victims—were involved in a way that made hangings seem about as healthful to the public as prostitution and cheap gin. (We have achieved the present hope of at last dispensing with legal murder only after decades of secluding executions from the public theater, making them impersonal, routine, boring acts of sanitary engineering.) But this character rushes disarmingly past his own muddle, leaving you helplessly confused about the intended point, though curious to know his view of lynchings.

"Point" is of course a visual metaphor, and McLuhan will have none of it. Stearn seems to think they're talking about how television reporting perpetuates the war, but McLuhan, while blandly nodding his head, clearly doesn't think the idea important or, for the moment, even true. He thinks TV "a disaster as far as Washington is concerned" because it involves people, creates absolute nausea, and so on. Fine, reasonable, comforting—but this proves the war would end if TV were shut off? Surely it proves just the contrary: without TV the war could go its way in the uninvolving newspapers, without popular opposition to "Washington" and its bloody business. McLuhan's "Oh yes" is priceless—Stearn and the innocent reader can happily suppose he means what they hope he means, but really he's only probing, spinning out his theory of *media*, not contemplating war or mass psychology. If Stearn wants to think that "connectedness, equality, sameness" refers to the civil rights movement, McLuhan has no objection; if Stearn is teasing him into saying something really outrageous, he is happy to oblige. But of course these words have nothing to do with civil rights. They're "technical" labels for perceptual assumptions, sense-ratios, but the misunderstanding doesn't matter so long as he can get in the clincher, the scrap of data ("hundreds of extra lines on the TV image") that proves he still knows what's what down at Bell Labs and still can dream anything into the grand design.

Yet it seems a little ungrateful to inquire too deeply into *what* such a resourceful voice is saying. McLuhan and his school are fallible analysts of intellectual history, as Kermode and Anthony Quinton have recently shown; his accounts of the present environment are suggestive but often wildly ill-considered; his projections of the electronic future are perhaps as crankish as his history. (To overlook in 1951 the coming of television, as he now admits he did in writing *The Mechanical Bride,* doesn't argue limitless prophetic powers, and in his present reluctance to relate his theories to the conditions of the drug culture he may be missing another boat.) One may agree with his main premises, which are mostly old friends anyway—yes, experience is metaphorical, forms of information are more potent than "content," our collective idea of reality does undergo large transformations as we live into new technologies—without thinking his the indispensable guidebook to the new disorder. But his style does reveal how the irritations and amusements of the present scene work on a mind formed by other environments. McLuhan stands for us, not least in acting out so many of our worst habits, and I want to launch some probes of my own into his literary presence and what it expresses.

A man's life is his own business, and I would not presume to intrude upon McLuhan's private self. But the "Marshall McLuhan" presented in the writings and talkings is a public figure and, like any public figure, in large part a deliberate fictional contrivance. *This* McLuhan is only too anxious to sever his present identity from the private biography, as he once told Eric Goldman:

> GOLDMAN: Here you are the son of Baptist parents, convert to Catholicism, a Canadian student of English literature, formerly an engineering student and now . . . .
> MCLUHAN: Oh, don't bother about that data.
> GOLDMAN: Why?
> MCLUHAN: It's all wrong! And, in any case, quite unnecessary.

Despite the disclaimer, it is a history of large conversions, from inherited Protestantism to Catholicism, from engineering to literature to some original synthesis of the two, from provincial Canadian (born in Alberta, educated in Manitoba) to metropolitan academic entrepreneur and world mastermind, from M.A. thesis on "George Meredith as a Poet and

Dramatic Parodist" to *Family Circle* piece on "What TV is Really Doing to Your Child" (the first and last entries in the hefty *Hot & Cool* bibliography), from Herbert Marshall McLuhan to just plain Marshall. For him this is "all wrong" or at least "quite unnecessary" to understanding how he lives now, but I'm not so sure.

While growing up in Buffalo, New York, I encountered a malicious myth about Canadians that may have been current in other border towns too. You learned to watch for cars with Ontario licenses so as to enjoy (you hoped) a glorious show of heedless, befuddled driving. Canadians, so the theory went, were mostly poor rubes, barred from civilizing influences by puritanical liquor laws and iron-jawed, incorruptible policemen—called "the Provincials" and rightly feared—quite unlike the raffish, all too human Irishmen and Germans and Poles who kept Buffalo only as lawful as it was in its nature to be. Thus the Canadians came over for a good time and, it being amply available, were dazzled into excesses fatal to what reason and mechanical competence they brought with them. Like the myth of American contempt for foreigners, this one had some small basis in truth.

Now for all I know, McLuhan may be an expert driver and a teetotaler; he can surely have little else in common with the desperate cutups from Port Colborne and St. Catherines and Crystal Beach who careen through my half-imaginary memories. But in their different ways he and they may have shared a sense of what a complex fate it is to be a Canadian in the shadow of the Image of Liberty that once was America if you didn't happen to live there yourself. Certainly McLuhan's view of Canada contains both affection and condescension:

> *Explorations* became an international magazine because it had something to say to the world, something new. It excited a lot of people. The idea that one could run something of real international interest and excite-

ment in a backward place like Canada charmed them. Canadians are all a very humble bunch. They take it for granted that everything they do must be second rate. Carpenter and I just blithely assumed that, since nearly everything in the world is second rate at best, there was no reason why we couldn't do something that was first rate here. So it happened.

This depends on believing both that Canada really is backward, so that *Explorations* seems all the more remarkable for coming from there, and that its backwardness is only an illusion of parochial self-doubt, since after all the magazine did happen in Canada and nowhere else. You accept "international" standards even as you insist that most things are second-rate everywhere. G. E. Stearn tells us that McLuhan's elocutionist mother was known as "the Ruth Draper of Canada," which might have seemed to imply that there was another Ruth Draper, the real one, for other places—while a boy from Sioux City might dream of saying something to America, a boy from Edmonton must have "something to say to the world."

The transmutation of Canada into the great globe itself is a mythic motif in McLuhanism. His fascination, approving or not, with "tribalism," the idea of the world as "global village" all electrically wired up to itself, seems a natural interest for a mind shaped by physical and cultural solitude. As in western American writers, you expect both a yearning for and a hostility to the great world of city culture; but for a Canadian, I suppose, that world isn't Montreal or Toronto, themselves tainted with the national sense of inferiority, but New York, Washington, imperial America as the pattern of provincial desire and the awful proof of where that desire finally leads. Certainly McLuhan's modern world is preeminently America, the land where media rule, where print culture was the only one achieved before the great plug-in came. He tells Stearn that "ear cultures" still exist in Russia, all backward or semiliterate societies (his examples are China and Ghana), Eskimo regions, "the Negro world," Castro's Cuba, the American South and (breathtakingly) England, though "the British are unaware of their auditory culture." Not much left. For "western visual man" read citified American man before his electric resurrections, and for "oral-aural man" read all those political or cultural antagonists (except the Eskimos?) who confront him at home and abroad. The subliminal bias isn't of course an expression of political or social doctrine—McLuhan doesn't much care whether it's the Negro world or the Klan that makes us sweat, just so long as we do so.

His ambivalence toward electric civilization seems quite genuine. It is the perfection of human interinvolvement, the abolition of open spaces and prairie silences, linear horizons and straight roads leading nowhere much, but it is also the hideous epitome of everything contemptible about an Americanized world, the cellophane and plastic brothel McLuhan icily visited in *The Mechanical Bride*. Electric America is where you want to go, and where you despise yourself for being. McLuhan sings the new environment by stressing just those qualities that, he well knows, will most distress those who cling to the old sense-ratios, and there is surely a touch of self-punishment in this:

> There is more diversity, less conformity under a single roof in any family than there is with the thousands of families in the same city. The more you create village conditions, the more discontinuity and division and diversity. The global village absolutely insures maximal disagreement on all points. It never occurred to me that uniformity and tranquility were the properties of the global village. It has more spite and envy. The spaces and times are pulled out from between people. A world in which people encounter each other in depth all the time.

> The tribal-global village is far more divisive—full of fighting—than any nationalism ever was. Village is fission, not fusion, in depth. People leave small towns to *avoid* involvement. The big city *lined* [lured?] them with its uniformity and impersonal milieu. They sought propriety and in the city, money is made by uniformity and repeatability. Where you have craftsmanlike diversity, you make art, not money. The village is not the place to find ideal peace and harmony. Exact opposite. Nationalism came out of print and provided an extraordinary relief from global village. I say we live in it.

Whatever the remarks about money and art may mean, the last sentences are clear enough. "We" must signify "we urbanized Americans," as opposed to the Russians and Ghanians and Alabamans who remain oral-aural, exempted from our ascent into typographic individualism and thus spared the painful heat of reentry, so to speak, into a tribal atmosphere that is only dangerous to those who have first left it.

But of course there's a more hopeful version of Global Village. In *Understanding Media* and *The Medium is the Massage* the tone is considerably less cautionary, and a strangely tentative moment may suggest why:

> One of the consequences of electronic environments is the total involvement of people in people. . . .
>
> Here perhaps my own religious faith has some bearing. I think of human charity as a total responsibility of all, for all. Therefore, my energies are directed at far more than mere political or democratic intent. Democracy as a by-product of certain technologies, like literacy and mechanical industry, is not something that I would take very seriously. But democracy as it belongs very profoundly with Christianity is something I take very seriously indeed.
>
> There have been many more religious men than I

> who have not made even the most faltering steps in
> this direction. Once I began to move in this direction,
> I began to see that it had profound religious meaning.
> I do not think it may job to point this out. For ex-
> ample, the Christian concept of the mystical body—
> all men as members of the body of Christ—this be-
> comes technologically a fact under electronic con-
> ditions. However, I would not try to theologize on the
> basis of my understanding of technology. I don't have
> a background in scholastic thought, never having been
> raised in any Catholic institution. Indeed, I have been
> bitterly reproached by my Catholic confrères for my
> lack of scholastic terminology and concepts.

This dismissal of political democracy as historical by-product smacks of the *National Review* brand of Catholic conservatism—typographical America figures as the old liberal state, with its concerns for those political and social definitions of human reality that Benjamin DeMott and Harold Rosenberg wish McLuhan could take more seriously. If the global village is the mystical body of Christ, then its tensions and animosities are only necessary ephemera, strains of discord that must be *felt,* however painfully, if one is ever to make out the ultimate harmony; order is not linear regularity but the simultaneous presence and relation of unlike things, as in old images of the divine economy. Remembering the fate of Titus Oates, I stop short of charging that McLuhan is engaged with Father Ong, Hugh Kenner, and the Fordham School of Communications in some sinister Popish Plot against secular consciousness. But his Catholicism does structure his more hopeful moods, as DeMott suggests in twitting him for setting up as "the constituted pardoner of this age—a purveyor of perfect absolution for every genuine kind of modern guilt."

It may be that the age can use a few pardoners, people who both recognize its guilts and preserve enough intellectual objectivity to deal with them sanely. I am not inevitably outraged by someone who wants to cheer me up. But McLuhan's claim that he preaches such objectivity is a little confusing:

> In his amusement born of rational detachment of [sic] his own situation, Poe's mariner in "The Descent into the Maelstrom" staved off disaster by understanding the action of the whirlpool. His insight offers a possible stratagem for understanding our predicament, our electrically-configured whirl.
>
> (*The Medium is the Massage*)

It's a favorite allusion, here dubbed in from the preface to *The Mechanical Bride*. But the present availability of such detachment is firmly denied elsewhere in *The Medium is the Massage:*

> Like easel painting, the printed book added much to the new cult of individualism. The private, fixed point of view became possible and literacy conferred the power of detachment, non-involvement. . . .
>
> The Renaissance Legacy.
>
> The Vanishing Point = Self Effacement.
> The Detached Observer
> No Involvement!
>
> The viewer of Renaissance art is systematically placed outside the frame of experience. . . .
>
> The instantaneous world of electric informational media involves all of us, all at once. No detachment or frame is possible.

We are to understand our predicament by doing what the predicament makes impossible, experiencing the electronic environment through a "rational detachment" that was created by and can be sustained only in perspective-print environments.

Detachment is the bad thing that lured oral-scribal man out of his medieval garden, yet it's what anyone will cultivate in the midst of bewildering cultural revolution. McLuhan the historical mapmaker is all Catholic and anti-individualist, yet he reaches for a strangely Protestant self-regulation when he contemplates himself *living* under the new dispensation.

The cast of McLuhan's mind, with its provincial cheekiness to the official culture it seeks to capture and its yearning for older, authoritarian models of belief, thus has much in common with those reactionary rebels—Joyce, Eliot, Pound, Wyndham Lewis—whom he so often invokes as intellectual patrons:

> Years ago, before I wrote the *Bride,* I had a moralistic approach to all environmental facts. I abominated machinery, cities, everything except the most Rousseauistic. Gradually, I became aware of how useless this was and I discovered that artists of the twentieth-century had a different approach and I adopted it.

It's his pleasantly old-fashioned idea of himself as artist, no doubt, that makes necessary his "metaphysical" style, the lapses of mere grammar and logic, the addiction to cute, gymnastic analogies, the discontent with clarity and consistency of topic. He finds his justification in such things as Cubism, Heisenbergian indeterminacy, *Finnegans Wake,* Toynbee, and these slightly dated excitements may seem a little out of phase with the evidence rather perfunctorily adduced from Burroughs, Jack Paar, the Beatles, *New Yorker* cartoons, or Op Art. Though he tries to keep up, he remains oddly out of it, involved with what's happening only insofar as it confirms what was predicted by the happenings of his own youth, forty years back. He admits he loathes *watching* TV, and nothing he says about (for example) pop music or the new film reflects much personal pleasure. His idea of fun—not one I can afford to ridicule—is surely sitting down with a good book, preferably not brand-new.

Thus it seems an error to accuse him of wanting to embrace the modern world in all its hideous charm. Rather I see him as a Secret Square, a grim figure something like Stephen Dedalus at Bella Cohen's, ill at ease with the scene except as it confirms his worst expectations and punishes his lingering nostalgia for older and seemlier ways. The trouble isn't that McLuhan exults in the electric environment but that, in his determination to make it *really* new, he conjures up a monstrosity he can take no pleasure in at all. If he opens doors to chaos, as Jonathan Miller worries, he seems no readier than anyone else his age to step through them himself. While he hopes that Global Village may be the mystical body, the Baptist keeps stirring around inside:

> Until writing was invented, man lived in acoustic space: boundless, directionless, horizonless, in the dark of the mind, in the world of emotion, by primordial intuition, by terror. Speech is a social chart of this bog.
>
> <div align="right">(<i>The Medium is the Massage</i>)</div>

This is the vision of *Finnegans Wake,* but without Joyce's unquenchable delight in the power of bog-life to rejuvenate the linguistic imagination. Maybe McLuhan is only trying to scare Dwight Macdonald here, but I suspect that a mind so quick to associate emotion with darkness and terror is already scared itself and needs some company. In short, I believe him both when he seems to welcome the new environment and when he protests that he doesn't welcome it in the least.

He's at his worst when he plays the sage, pronouncing organized conceptual plenitude upon a world that would otherwise be unbearable in its randomness, a Virgil in search of other Dantes than just himself. But if we would locate our infernal regions elsewhere, in that very consciousness of personal and collective failure he so insistently excludes from his scheme, we might do well, in dismissing his pretensions, not to dismiss the phenomena he calls to our attention. He himself, in his literary presence, is a modern phenomenon, and a particularly pleasant one. He is not a serious man—indeed it's one of his virtues that in some moods he would take this as a compliment. Rather he's a modern type of the Enthusiast, the man who (like some Swiftian Projector) has found the right "approach" at last and wants very badly to share his great secret with the world. He loves the sound of words like *absolutely, totally, perfect, exact, entire, complete,* as well as ones like *fantastic, amazing, tremendous;* and we all know that voice and have felt inner dismay as it approaches across the noisy room, grips our elbow, and solves the universe before our eyes. But if the solutions keep changing, that may be because the problems do too, and there are possibilities of delight as well as dismay in the spectacle of perpetual mental motion and an amiable indifference to one's own comic value. It would be miraculous if a "surround" as fragmented, discontinuous, and irrational as he says ours is *could* be adequately explicated by a mind so infatuated with historical patterns and universal correspondences, and so innocently committed to instrumental solutions. But the McLuhan style, with its suprarational agility, its hunger to know just enough about everything to escape ever having to shut up, its saving power to forget what it just said, does in a funny way convey the feel of experience nowadays and demonstrate some of the skills it takes to keep going.

Indignation or horror is not the best response to McLuhan. He once dismissed hostile critics by observing that "many people would rather be villains than nitwits," and one suspects that he quite enjoys the lurid roles he's so often cast in; but his own literary presence is hardly that menacing. He would be at home in a Dickens novel or a play of Shaw's, and there you would never mistake him for a villain.

*"The New West" is largely a complaint about the abuse of literary evidence to serve an at least dubious theory, even though a generous motive stands behind it. Leslie Fiedler was I think trying to imagine American Indians seriously and unsentimentally, a worthy effort indeed. But another intention, having to do with social marginality and cultural revolt generally, was also in play in* The Return of the Vanishing American, *as it was in American universities like Fiedler's and my own in 1968; and for all my sympathy for the effort, it seemed to me important to get things straight, which I felt Fiedler's argument rather sensationally failed to do.*

# The New West
(1968)

$L$ESLIE Fiedler's new book completes the "venture in literary anthropology" begun with *Love and Death in the American Novel* and continued in *Waiting for the End*. Having dealt with "*eros* and *thanatos*" and with "the hope of apocalypse and its failure," he now turns to "the Indian," which sounds anticlimactic and I'm afraid finally is so, taking *The Return of the Vanishing American* as a whole critical performance. The significance of the venture I leave to the American Studies people to worry out—part of the fun of reading Fiedler (and of being him, I dare say) is imagining their solemn outrage. I am more interested in figuring out why so lively and adventurous a book leaves me feeling disappointed and annoyed.

By now the objections to Fiedler's procedures are virtually standardized. He can be careless about little accuracies (*What Are We Doing in Vietnam?* is a good question but not the title of a Mailer novel) and silly with his analogies ("those first hippies of the Western world, Raleigh, Marlowe, and company"), and his habit of melodramatizing history will not be to everyone's taste: "It is only a step from thinking of the West as madness to regarding madness as the true West, but it took the long years between the end of the fifteenth century and the middle of the twentieth to learn to take that step." He likes to work with a stacked deck, too, as when he argues blandly that "the real opposite of nostalgic is psychedelic, the reverse of remembering is hallucinating, which means that, insofar as the New Western is truly New, it, too, must be psychedelic." The force of "real" and "truly" is worth pondering, and one relishes those fussy little commas toward the end, with their air of nice rational precision. Anyone who thought the reverse of remembering was forgetting will feel pretty baffled; but Fiedler is an incorrigible rascal, and to forbid him his tricks would deprive us of the fine insights he sometimes has up his sleeve.

The insights in *The Return of the Vanishing American* are, however, achieved at a pretty high price. For example, the very interesting chapter called "The World Without a West" pairs off two views of American Indians held around 1600—Montaigne's, that the new men in the west *were* men, culturally different from Europeans but human and humanly important, fit objects for anthropological curiosity and maybe even covert primitivist admiration, and Shakespeare's, that the Indian (Caliban = cannibal = Carib) is a dark subhuman enemy, a bestial rapist who threatens the White pieties of marriage, feminized culture, and order generally. It probably does no good to protest that *The Tempest* is not "about" Caliban, that in pursuing a large and complex dramatic purpose Shakespeare found current lore about Indian cannibalism and sexual prepotence useful in imagining a figure of brute passion and (which Fiedler doesn't mention) low comic cunning, just as he did lore about blackamoors and amphibians. *The Tempest* is *not* a "violent attack on the whole Indian race, disguised as a Mystery Play," nor does Fiedler's point about the mythic value of Indians really demand that it be taken as such; it's just a provocative remark, one that comes all the easier for Fiedler's lack of interest in literary works as whole expressive objects, his concern, like some crazed Ph.D. candidate, only for what they *contain* that fits the investigative category. If you are looking for Indians in the Renaissance you will find Caliban; just so, if

## The New West

you're looking for certain myths you will be surprised and irritated when they're not there—Fiedler calls Irving obtuse for not having put some Indians into "The Legend of Sleepy Hollow" and Twain disingenuous for pretending not to notice "the woodland romance between the White Man and the Indian" that was really what irked him about Cooper. (When someone doesn't see what you want seen, you conclude that a secret fear is being covered up; we owe lots of nonsense about Jane Austen, for example, to this kind of reasoning.) By a happy chance, Fiedler's own story "The First Spade in the West" suits his critical purposes better—the right ingredients are *there*, and he cites it three times.

But even this sort of thing, which I don't assume Fiedler is unaware of or unamused by, doesn't account for my reservations. For all the hocus-pocus, his exploration of his main myth—the enmity between men (secret anarchists and escape-artists) and women (all-possessive, castrating, culture-mongering Jewish-mother types)—is intriguing and often subtle. If the myth seems a little large to be just American, it gets adequately domesticated through a four-fold division into the sub-myths of The Runaway Slave (Rip Van Winkle), Love in the Woods (Pocahontas and John Smith—the *false* myth), The White Woman with a Tomahawk (Hannah Duston the Indian-killer), and The Good Companions in the Wilderness (Alexander Henry and Wawatam, Natty Bumpo and Chingachgook). These are traced with fine ingenuity through the disguises and sentimentalizations by which we have tried to veil their darker implications, as in the wonderful demonstration of how Pocahontas became both an angelic She-Redeemer and the Indian Maid of smutty folklore and satiric anti-western fiction. For Fiedler, one of whose purposes is to defend the mythopoeic gift against tenderfoot snobs like James, Eliot, and Leavis, the patterns add up to "the archetypal Westerner whose legend is the essential myth of America":

Henry and Natty and Rip together constitute the image of the runaway from home and civilization whom we long to be when we are our most authentic selves; Dame Van Winkle and Hannah and Eve add up to the image of his dearest enemy, spokesman for the culture and the European inheritance he flees; Wawatam and Bampico and Chingachgook and the Old Serpent himself make up the Good Companion, representative of an alternative past embracing which he can achieve a future available to no European. Yet it is a melancholy myth the three define, for all its hopefulness; since the Indian, midwife and mother to the New Son whose father is his Old World self, dies giving birth—"vanishes" without a surviving bodily heir in order to leave room for his spiritual offspring.

You either like such talk or you don't, I suppose; for me the beauty of Fiedler's Way is not in such broad vistas but in surprising glimpses of particular literary occasions, passages in Meriwether Lewis's journal, Thoreau on Hannah Duston, the ending of *Torrents of Spring*. Fiedler doesn't explain our whole history quite as tidily as he pretends to, but he helps us with it, moment by moment.

But like a now familiar kind of academician, he's overanxious that his view of the past also seem up-to-date, Relevant to Our Times, not just in showing how we got that way but in prescribing what to do next. The last chapters of *The Return of the Vanishing American* stress "return," arguing that for all the wit and point of the satiric Anti-Westerns of John Barth, James Leo Herlihy, Thomas Berger, Leonard Cohen, and others, the West is really used up as a literary subject and setting, as it's used up in a reality of superhighways, motels, and gift shops; with that understood, and after a welcome debunking of science-fiction and a dismaying celebration of Ken Kesey as our authentic novelist, he can at last make the pitch one feared all along was coming:

# The New West

> If a myth of America is to exist in the future, it is incumbent on our writers, no matter how square and scared they may be in their deepest hearts, to conduct with the mad just such a dialogue as their predecessors learned long ago to conduct with the aboriginal dwellers in the actual Western wilderness. It is easy to forget, but essential to remember, that the shadowy creatures living scarcely imaginable lives in the forests of Virginia once seemed as threatening to all that good Europeans believed as the acid-head or the borderline schizophrenic on the Lower East Side now seems to all that good Americans have come to believe in its place.

That final sentence (the last in the book) rings hollow with its careful parallelisms and balances and its ponderous instructive tone; it's often the slow-curve artists who show you a lot of arm, and the rhetorical wind-up makes you wonder if Fiedler really trusts his stuff here. When critics begin to tell writers what is incumbent on them, something is wrong.

A program for redeeming and perpetuating a myth seems odd coming from someone who stakes so much on myth as the articulation of *unconfessed* assumptions and desires. Surely the last thing that can preserve the mythic force of American or any other literature is a calculated artistic regimen for *making* new cultural cases do the work of old ones. Fiedler is like the dean of a newly-established college where I once worked, who appointed a committee to invent some "traditions" for the place; it's one thing to say that "The 'New Race' which D. H. Lawrence foresaw (and toward which, with or without benefit of literature, we are moving at an astonishing rate) demands New Myth," but quite another to legislate, more or less in cold blood, what that myth shall be.

A literary anthropologist should be the first to insist that a kind of literature doesn't lose its mythic force just because it's not being written, right now, somewhere down the street. It's admirable of Fiedler to be concerned about the New

Savages and to insist that we have literary commerce—intercourse, he might say—with them; but of course we'll do that anyway, not in order to preserve "the essential myth of America" (even if Fiedler is right about what that is) but because they are real people, interesting and disturbing ones who may help us understand the present and what it could lead to and whose experience matters because it is human experience. In the process of imagining their lives we indeed may find some affinity to our best imaginings of Indians, the alien others who challenge us to consider alternative histories and new selves in the present; but serious art always effects alteration of consciousness, and it needn't be *about* alteration of consciousness in Fiedler's sense to do its job.

Fiedler's idea of myth is dangerous to his anthropological intentions:

> It is only a dream, perhaps, this vision of love and reconciliation between the races whose actual history is oppression and hate; but it is a dream we do not willingly surrender, our dearest myth, sustained by the faith Thoreau himself expresses at the end of the chapter in which he recounts the legend of Henry and Wawatam: "But in my dream ideal justice was at length done . . . and I was unspeakably soothed and rejoiced . . . because in dreams we never deceive ourselves, nor are deceived. . . . Our truest life is when we are in dreams awake."

"Dream" is a perilous metaphor, and Thoreau's ambiguous last sentence comes awkwardly into Fiedler's context: do we find our truest life when we conduct our waking selves in accordance with the justice we learn in dreams, or when we extend dreaming into waking life, treating it *as if it were* a place of justice rather than the unjust place reason and observation report it to be? One hopes the former, but without being sure that Fiedler always sees it that way—the vision is *"our* dearest myth" all right, but how dear and soothing and rejoiceful can it be to the Indians, or to blacks, whom Fiedler irritatingly keeps treating as Indians in disguise? The book has an epigraph from Lévi-Strauss, stressing his compassionate concern for the dying peoples he has worked with and (by implication) insisting on the integrity of their styles of organizing their experience, whose validity and dignity is independent of our usually patronizing and distorting ways of apprehending them. Fiedler knows this, and certainly he has respect and compassion for the Indians, but his anthropology requires that they mostly be figures of *our* myths, creatures of our own guilts and dreams, whose mythic status as psychic redeemers is only made possible by an actual history of genocidal horror. One wonders how the acid-heads and borderline schizophrenics feel about becoming the mythic matter of the New Western—is *that* the best way to take their experience seriously?

In short, I don't think that Fiedler's way of treating myth is as easily transferable into prescriptive program as he wants it to be. His methods do damage not just to literature, by breaking up whole works to salvage the "authentic" fragment, but to life, by making it only a kind of *materia mythica* to be arranged and manipulated without entering very deeply into the particular experiences that compose it. He doesn't mean to do this, and his career is a deserved and salutary rebuke to those who would insulate art from its human motives and consequences; but *The Return of the Vanishing American,* for all its admirable intentions and its pleasures and illuminations, is finally bad medicine.

# CRY WOLFE

*Like McLuhan and Fiedler, Tom Wolfe was in the 1960s and '70s applying essentially academic modes of analysis to the radically altered terms of American social life outside the academy. (If "academic" seems an odd label for Wolfe's game, remember that he started out as a graduate student in American Studies at Yale, and that from behind the swags and festoons of his style a cool sociological eye is always looking things over.) I imagine that Wolfe took his own theoretical system less seriously than McLuhan and Fiedler did theirs, and in the following two pieces I was ready to welcome relaxation of the barriers between the intellectual and the popular.* The Electric Kool-Aid Acid Test *seemed to me in many ways an impressive rendering of a new life that most of us as yet knew little about, but even there I saw signs of what would be dismayingly clearer in* Radical Chic & Mau-Mauing the Flak Catcher, *defective powers of sympathy and generosity and a rather sly way of titillating our fears of the new even while accommodating our most reactionary responses to it.*

# No Country for Old Men
(1969)

*H*ARD as is to take Tom Wolfe seriously, whether as stylist or swami of culture, his version of America in the sixties is worth some thought. He himself is a phenomenon of the decade, a journalist whose talents would earlier have been flattened out and institutionalized by the copy editors of *Time* or some lesser slickness; *Esquire* and the *Herald Tribune* in fact brought him to light in their scurryings after new formats and tones as circulations declined, and his mannerisms did seem to be what the age demanded. For what must to him have seemed an enchanted few years, everyone read and talked about his portraits of freakishness, in pop-society, the teen-age underworld, the T-shirt cultures of the backlands. Since then, the fun has worn a little thin, but the *The Electric Kool-Aid Acid Test,* his book on the Ken Kesey circle, is in many ways a successful new departure, and it's worth asking who we are when we read Wolfe, what sense of contemporary America and ourselves he makes available.

First some propositions about his way of operating, for later elaboration. (1) It is pointless to ask what he *means* by it all, what intellectual or moral positions he speaks from. His method proliferates points of view, plays with the reader's prior assumptions, implies attitudes that are then reneged on or thrown away. He is, indeed, a rather broad caricature of "modernism" in action. (2) He always has in mind an audience that's a little less "so" than the persons or styles he writes about. We are less vulgar than his vulgarians, less hip than his sophisticates, less obsessed than his fanatics, which is to say that we are the stereotypical reader of *Esquire* or the *Herald Tribune,* anxious to be in the know about Baby Jane Holzer or stock-car racing or topless shoeshine girls or the drug scene, yet inwardly sure that we know better, just as Wolfe does. (3) But Wolfe has considerable contempt for our thinking that we know better, and he likes to insist that popular culture, commercial or folk, is a good deal more alive and authentic than the arts and values we think "serious." (4) Thus he pointedly ridicules conventional intellectuality and its ponderous professors, treats politics as a stupid and unreal game, and takes social problems to be the fictions of apocalypse-mongers; his message is "Enjoy." (5) But we, his readers, are in his view debarred by age or social status or inherited shibboleths of taste and morality or just plain cowardice from enjoying what the young, the provincials, the proles (a favorite word) enjoy so directly and innocently. Our pleasure will always be at one remove, a little self-conscious and patronizing. The contradictions in all this are worth exploring.

Youth and Age is, overtly or subliminally, Wolfe's major theme. Many of his subjects are themselves young, and those who (like Ken Kesey) aren't getting any younger are usually physically imposing, reckless, rebellious, or adept with machinery, so that they can easily *mean* "youth" to prudent old incompetents. (At worst, they are Falstaffianly interested in the young, like Murray The K.) In a larger way, Wolfe sees the received culture itself as old and feeble; his people are making their own styles and roles, virtually without regard for the established order, which in truth is not established at all but subject to continuous revolutionary change in a time when even children are affluent beyond the dreams of their grandfathers.

This is, of course, a large subject just now. After two centuries of sentimentalizing childhood and extending its duration farther and farther past puberty, we discover that our young aren't especially happy about being old-style children—though we then can only rather helplessly complain that this is childish of them. To give Wolfe credit, he never mentions the Generation Gap, that boring idea; he's interested in how the youth, or the crypto-youth, go about inventing their own societies, how their styles try to generate a felt mutuality and trust, a sense of communal permanence that might withstand the flow of time toward the age—by convention, thirty—at which one becomes unarguably grown up. The young in one another's arms grow older, though neither they nor the indignant scarecrows looking on may notice, and Wolfe is admirably gentle with them, as he expects us not to be.

But Wolfe mostly has his eye not on the young themselves, who seem to be doing all right, but on the troubled middle-aged reader. A climactic moment in *The Electric Kool-Aid Acid Test* brings the matter to the surface. At the last of Kesey's acid test parties, when he and his disciples, The Merry Pranksters, are rather showily enacting the transcendent oneness they seek with each other and the All, Kesey's children are brought in by their mother and are understandably terrified by this three A.M. spookiness, from which even tolerably hip grown-ups are fleeing in embarrassed panic:

> One of them is crying, only it is like a scream. That's all you hear in here, it's eerie. . . Faye and the kids and Mountain Girl and Sunshine and all the Pranksters in a tight circle with Kesey. They all hold hands and close their eyes. Silence. Then the scream again.

ARCHETYPICAL! MIND POWER!

Then a voice from one of the clumps of people by the wall, some girl, with a spondee voice like a Ouija medium:

"The—child—is—cry-ing—Do—some-thing—for—the—child—first—"

Kesey says nothing. His eyes are shut tight. The high keening sound rises from the circle with the kid's scream weaving through it. Fantastic mind power crackle—Goldhill registers the energy.

THEY'RE ALMOST

But the girl on the side doesn't let up: "See—a-bout—the—child—A—child—is—cry-ing—That's—all—that's—hap-pening—A—child—is—cry-ing—and—no—one—is—do-ing—any-thing—a-bout—it—"

ALMOST HAVE IT—PRESQUE VU!

"—Why—is—the—child—cry-ing—Doesn't—an-y-bo-dy—care?—"

FEEL IT! THE VIBRATION LEVEL!

Kesey looks up. The spot hits him in the face. The Pranksters release hands. The music starts up. The Anonymous Artists of America play a low rock 'n' roll version of Pomp and Circumstance with drum flourishes . . .

THE ACID TEST GRADUATION

In asking what this elaborately rendered moment might mean, one could think first of simple indignation. It's not good for children to stay up too late, especially when they are being scared silly by what even some adults found a grotesque spectacle. There's Dad, dressed up in cape and leotards like Captain Marvel, doing incomprehensible things and *not even noticing* them and their terror in the night! This reaction, which I suppose few can resist entirely, then feeds into a general dislike and fear of what Kesey was up to, or a dismissal of it all as a simple-minded, gauche excess—like the judge who called him "a childish ass, an egotist who never grew up" and then let him out on bail.

Yet if Wolfe's vignette lets one get even with Kesey for being such an outrageous freak, it also makes room for an adversary view of "a child is crying." The girl's "spondee" enunciation seems mechanical and lifeless (one is invited to wonder what *she* was on); her concern seems only the impersonating of a reflex moralism; her assumption that a fearful child takes priority over everything seems at least dubious. What if Kesey had been finishing the Sistine Ceiling, saving the earth from colliding with Saturn, graduating from Yale? Should he then have stopped because his kids were crying? What he was doing was important, at least to him and a few others, the most important thing he or maybe anyone had ever done; his children should be in on the great moment, even at the expense of their usual schedule and their emotional tranquility, as the children of the Apollo 11 crew were late getting home (and perhaps were cranky?) after seeing their papas fly off to the moon. Some adult purposes may be more adult than others, but it's not the crying child that determines whether Kesey's behavior was shocking or asinine; the girl's most telling line is not "a child is crying" but "that's all that's happening," which evidently seemed true to many others present.

This is not to speculate about Kesey's sanity or moral sense but to ask what Wolfe has in mind for us. At such a moment possibilities of feeling come together in intriguing confusion: the curiously deadened voice of conventional moral sentiment collides with the curiously indifferent intensity of religious ecstasy and chemical revelation, and neither voice can hear the other. But for Wolfe's reader the chips are down, and it may be the last spin of the wheel—the book is ending, and his own kids have been acting a little oddly of late. "A child is crying" gives this reader a way out, not through some embarrassingly square hostility to hippie drug-fiend weirdos but through a less evidently conventional "human" pity and concern for neglected innocence. Wolfe leaves this door wide open by dwelling on the girl's protests, but I seem to detect some contempt for anyone who needs to exit through it.

Wolfe's implicit drama of generational conflict considers the play of opposing styles within an affluent society that uses consumer taste, rather than class and interest in the old sense, as its organizing principle. His America has raised incomes and cheapened goods to the point where every person, from Hugh Hefner to the humblest ranch-houser, has the power to create his own material kingdom with himself as sole monarch and arbiter, the "status sphere " (or "statusphere," or "statussphere"—Wolfe keeps changing the spelling) as do-it-yourself Versailles. The teen-age Hair Boys at Los Angeles drive-ins dress and coif themselves into charismatic roles like seventeenth-century courtiers; a car-customizer in his garage is a modern Tiepolo; Phil Spector, the rock-record magnate, is at twenty-three the Cellini (or Chesterfield, or Jefferson, or Rossetti) of adolescent America. Instant Max Weber is less intrusive in Wolfe's later writings, but he's always alert to the symbolism of role-playing in the subcultures he describes, and the word "Sociology" on the back of the soft-cover edition of *The Kandy-Kolored Tangerine-Flake Streamline Baby* is a fair enough guide to the drugstore book buyer.

The jokes lurking in his own roles are perfectly evident to Wolfe, and he well knows that others see the world differently. In the preface to *The Pump House Gang* he bemusedly describes his participation in a Princeton symposium on "The Style of the Sixties," where the other participants, earnest types like Günter Grass and Allen Ginsberg, kept bringing up political oppression, police statism, war, poverty, alienation. "'What are you talking about?' I said. 'We're in the middle of a . . . Happiness Explosion!'" Like McLuhan, whom he has written well about, Wolfe dismisses politics and social issues as the old games of solemn intellectuals, to him invariably objects of pity or scorn. He describes with glee the Pump House surfers dropping in on the Watts riots "stoned out of their hulking gourds":

> Watts was a blast, and the Pump House gang was immune to the trembling gourd panic rattles of the L. A. *Times*. . . . Immune! . . . . Artie and John had a tape-recorder and decided they were going to make a record called "Random Sounds from the Watts Riots." They drove right into Watts . . . and there was blood on the streets and roofs blowing off the stores and all these apricot flames and drunk Negroes falling through the busted plate glass of the liquor stores. Artie got a nice recording of a lot of Negroes chanting "Burn, baby, burn."

The young tourists were well received by some of the natives ("Come on, man, it's a party and it's free"), though there were other random sounds too: "A car full of Negroes *did* stop them and say, Whitey, Geed'um, and all that stuff, but one of the guys in Gary's car just draped a pistol he had out the window and the colored guys went off." Nothing a properly equipped teen-ager couldn't handle.

Now one may not be quite ready to see Watts as a happiness explosion, and Wolfe's dead-pan mimicry of the kids' own argot makes available all the irony one can use. But *he* won't use it—indeed, his scorn for "serious" social concern makes the passage a virtual endorsement of the attitudes it reports. It's too good a joke, on the cops and the worried burghers and the L. A. *Times* and the comic-opera blacks, for Wolfe to let it become a political drama of conflicting minds struggling for adequate self-representation. If the guy with the pistol wasn't a little scared, if the black kids didn't say "Come on, man, it's a party" with some mixture of shame and hatred, I'd be very much surprised.

But for Wolfe, politics and its human implications are mere bullshit:

> The main trouble with the Vietnam Day Committee was that they couldn't see beyond the marvelous political whoopee they had cooked up. Why should they? From where they were looking in the fall of 1965, they were about to sweep the country. Berkeley, the New Left, the Free Speech Movement, Mario Savio, the Rebel Generation, the Student Revolution, in which students were going to take over the universities, like in Latin America, and drive some fire up the clammy rectum of American life—you could read about it in all the magazines. And if you don't believe it, come here and watch us, Mr. Jones—and so forth.

To this way of seeing it, it was a howl for Kesey and the Pranksters to show up at the Vietnam Day rally in military uniforms, with guns and the Bus fixed up like a tank and all that stuff, and a pity that the Hell's Angels didn't make the scene after all. The open irony Wolfe withholds from the Pump House Gang isn't withheld from political protest, and for one who finds the evanescence of other styles a pleasant confirmation of his sociology, he takes an oddly stern view of the evanescence of *political* styles.

I blame Wolfe not for wanting to think that public concerns, and their rhetoric, are trivial or fraudulent—that is sometimes salutary—but for insinuating that the reader in the suburbs or wherever is somehow supported in his own indifference to social and political justice by the very different indifference of the teenagers and proles and the deracinated impresarios who manipulate and use them. Not that Wolfe's devices aren't cunning. He is interested in power, not as a political property but a personal one; his heroes, as I said earlier, are usually men of impressive physical or psychic force, strong men who have mastered difficult skills or powerful machines like motorcycles or souped-up cars, and whose personal style asserts an imperviousness to fear or the complex social delicacies. And the image of such men grabs the respectable reader quite literally by the balls:

> The genteel suburban kid rides his bicycle over to the gas station and there in the grease pit area where they lubricate the cars the hard rocks are hunkered down telling jokes about pussy, with an occasional clinical reference to bowel movements and crepitation. And oh christ don't you remember their forearms with the basilic veins wrapped around them like surgical tubes, gorged with the unattainable lower-class hard-rock power that any moment is going to look up and *spot* us . . . genteel little pudding kids.

Well, yes, this is an acute joke as far as it goes, but I doubt that it explains as much as it seems to. Some intellectuals no doubt do hanker after "Low Rent stuff" because it made them feel so scared and sissified in the formative years, and some middle-class citizens perhaps do lack social generosity because their non-physical lives, and associated fears of sexual inadequacy, make the prole world seem personally menacing. But the point is scored without convincing me that it adequately explains why, for example, the Hell's Angels are such troubling objects of thought—surely they mean something larger than our adolescent nightmare of class-determined impotence.

Wolfe's theory is that there's a vitality in the "low" world that we hunger for but (poor geldings!) can't embrace without making fools of ourselves:

> Once it was power that created high style. But now high styles come from low places, from people who have no power, who slink away from it, in fact, who are marginal, who carve out worlds for themselves in the nether depths, in tainted "undergrounds." The Rolling Stones, like rock and roll itself and the twist—they come out of the netherworld of modern teen-age life, out of what was for years the marginal outcast corner of the world of art, photography, populated by poor boys, pretenders. . . . Teen-agers, bohos, camp culturati, photographers—they have won by default, because, after all, they *do* create styles. And now the Other Society goes to them for styles, like the decadenti of another age going down to the wharves in Rio to find those raw-vital devils, damn their potent hides, those proles, doing the Tango. Yes! Oh my God, those raw-vital proles!

This is an early attempt, from *The Kandy-Kolored* (etc.) *Baby,* and it doesn't quite work. High styles have been coming from low places for a lot longer than Wolfe admits—see, for example, Huizinga on the vogue of pastoral in late-medieval court societies—and of course low styles come from high places too. Wolfe's instances—the Rolling Stones and so on—may have marginal origins, but it seems hard to believe that their arts are in any simple way expressive of those origins;

they're equally expressive of how someone apprehended and used styles that were already commercially viable and ready to be exploited. Wolfe punishes the "Other Society" by doing exactly what he scorns it for doing, sentimentalizing the "netherworlds" below it.

In Ken Kesey Wolfe found a better sociological subject. Kesey is no prole but the son of a prosperous Oregon businessman, an athletic college boy who adopted Low Rent styles as (in some part) a satiric weapon against his peers, and most of the Pranksters were middle-class dropouts rather than authentically marginal people. (Their jokes were often quite literary, their myths based on snippets from survey courses in Western—or Eastern—Civilization; some seem to have been getting an allowance from their parents.) Kesey offered physical and psychic strength without raising tricky questions about social origins; the point of the Wolfeian hero is not where he comes from but the way in which he invents his style and then lives it, and Kesey was blessedly not doing his thing with an eye on *Vogue,* Ed Sullivan, or the Top Ten charts. Far more than Wolfe's earlier subjects, Kesey was bright and well aware of the mythic expressiveness of his behavior, and, despite his moment of overreaching in expecting the Beatles to recognize him as a peer, not much interested in promoting himself outside the circle of his good companions. Pranksterism, far from taking its own art and its commercial possibilities seriously, sought not to startle and intrigue conventional taste into buying something but to be truly and unforgivably offensive. If Kesey's sense of his relation to the "Other World" grew darker and more paranoid as the cops finally closed in, it was all great fun for a while.

Kesey's myth-making used materials familiar to modern teen-age America—school buses, tape recorders, Kool-Aid, drugs, cartoon superheroes like Superman and The Flash—in the service of higher ends, which Wolfe almost accepts as a search for spiritual community through shared religious illumination, the withdrawal of the Aware from the unaware mass life all around them. Though he sometimes exploits many of his readers' hopes for an exposé of Hot Times in Drugsville, the whole effect of *The Electric Kool-Aid Acid Test* is to make the role of drugs in the Pranksters' experience seem almost incidental. Acid and grass were part of their stock of materials, but so were Day-Glo paint and electronic devices and internal combustion engines, and to them the aims mattered more than the instruments. Wolfe does play with a tragic shape in Kesey's career—his growing authoritarianism, hubris leading to paranoia, the breakdown or death of some of the Pranksters; and we are, I suppose, free to attribute the pattern to the stuff they were taking. But if the relations between Kesey and his people were in some ways damaged by drugs, they remain recognizable versions of personal relations in a community that seems to have been no more unstable than many straight groups.

And that, I think, is Wolfe's best, and trickiest, point about America now. The freakiest behavior, the scariest challenge to the *Herald Tribune* reader, is only a new permutation of that reader's world, another use of its own materials. Read one way, this is a valuable idea, since it helps explain one's mixed feelings about the Youth Scene, the New People. It is exciting to see old things put to new purposes, it's about time they were; and yet one wishes the purposes were even newer, the materials a little less junky and apt to break. Those dying generations do die—literally, like some of the Pranksters, or just figuratively, drifting back disheveled from The Territory to serve out their time in the old settlements. Read another way, however, Wolfe's point gives too much comfort to the oldsters, permitting us to suppose that the new isn't really *that* new and scary. He remarks that there was some of the air of an old-style college weekend about the Pranksters' doings, letting us reflect that the alcohol scene of our own youth (whenever that was) was pretty wild and silly and violent and pathetic too, though of course we dressed neater and had to work harder for sex. Whether or not he believes it—who can say?—Wolfe caters to such hopes rather shamelessly. We won't learn much from the Pranksters, or any of Wolfe's lesser creatures, if we think they're just differently costumed versions of the kids down at the old Tappa Keg House; if that is really all they are, it's a great pity.

# Radical Chic
(1971)

Tom Wolfe has the great journalist's knack of finding large subjects in small places, but he can't resist reducing them to the scale of his own taste. In *Radical Chic & Mau-Mauing the Flak Catcher* he uses the Leonard Bernsteins' "party" for the Panther 21 and the troubles of California anti-poverty programs to play variations on a serious theme, the dynamics of confrontation between oppressed people and well-intentioned privilege. But in both cases Wolfe finally achieves complacent if elegant minification.

"Mau-Mauing the Flak Catchers," the shorter piece, asks no one to worry much about social injustice or its violent potentialities. Wolfe suggests that anti-poverty programs, which assume that assistance is productive only if funneled through existing ghetto power-structures (which to Wolfe can only mean *gangs*), actually create fictitious power-structures. His San Francisco blacks have learned that you get government money by going down to some office and demanding it; if they can abuse and threaten the bureaucrat into fearing for his life or his manhood, they get the money, since his sentimental premise is that the worst, most menacing element *has* power in the ghetto. If they really scare him, they must be the ones he's looking for.

Now no one has much power in ghettos, Wolfe claims, and it's a rare Mau-Mau who means what he says. Most such demands are ritual bluffs, which pay off only if they can penetrate the counter-ritual of the Flak Catcher, the functionary with no bursary power who listens sympathetically but does nothing unless he's terrorized into calling up the real boss. If he can hold out until the Mau-Maus go away, he has probably won, since they are mostly too lazy and dumb, too easily gratified by making The Man sweat, to come back the next day and squeeze him some more.

Wolfe's tone represents this as a harmless charade, all the more amusing because it degrades and humiliates everyone concerned, his prepotent but child-like and shiftless blacks no less than his gutless, time-serving, sexually anxious white bureaucrats. To the couturier's eye all is revealed by a contrast like that between the Flak Catchers' Hush Puppies ("they cost about $4.99, and the second time you move your toes, the seams split and the tops come away from the soles") and the puissant footwear of the Mau-Maus ("the straps on the sandals look like they were made from the reins on the Budweiser draft horses," "a cordovan brogue with a sole sticking out like a rock ledge"). But a less doggedly sartorial theory of human nature than Wolfe's might find both his blacks and his bureaucrats blatant stereotypes, and his cozy estimate of the importance of ritual confrontation—"It got to be an American custom, like talk shows, Face the Nation, marriage, marathon encounters, or zoning hearings"—trivializes a difficult social problem even as it sneers at the suburban verities it pretends to soothe us with. Any sociologist knows that motives aren't less real and compelling for being ritualized, and any newspaper reader knows that more goes on in ghettos than Wolfe's comic-opera Mau-Mauing.

"Radical Chic," the longer essay, presents the psychodynamics of confrontation with even more malice. Again Wolfe can't keep his imaginative hands off the costumes, decor, and cuisine that here are asked to measure the incongruity between Upper East Side domestic style and the cause of Justice for the Panthers:

> In fact, there is a certain perfection as the first Black Panther rises within a Park Avenue living room to lay the Panthers' ten-point program on New York Society in the age of Radical Chic. Cox is silhouetted—well, about nineteen feet behind him is a white silk shade with an Empire scallop over one of the windows overlooking Park Avenue. Or maybe it isn't silk but a Jack Lenor Larsen mercerized cotton, something like that, lustrous but more subtle than silk. The whole image, the white shade and the Negro by the piano silhouetted against it, is framed by a pair of button-green velvet curtains, pulled back.

That "certain perfection" is worth pondering, even apart from the hard-hat resentment of "Park Avenue" and "New York Society" it so delicately strokes. It's not quite that easy to see a "big, tall" man silhouetted against even a Bernstein-sized window nineteen feet behind him; and how many of the ninety-odd people in that "big, wide" room could have seen Don Cox from exactly that angle anyway? Did Wolfe see this "image" himself? (Can they have invited *him?*) Even if he did see it, has a merely verbal particularity ("Jack Lenor Larsen mercerized cotton") perhaps created a spurious "perfection" for our benefit, the objects sounding so plausibly there that one doesn't want to question the locations and meanings ascribed to them?

This is a complaint not about Wolfe's honesty—we by now allow for such novelistic strategies in journalism—but about the narrowness of his art, in which data, observed or invented, is "composed" so as to support a prior theory. For Wolfe, the scene in the Bernsteins' living room is required to serve his pet sociological thesis, here called *nostalgie de la boue,* the gentry's hankering after a muddy proletarian primitivism. He shows us cultivated parvenu Jews, torn between cherished new right-wing life-styles and the left-wing politics of their own oppressed history, ludicrously confused about how to take Black Revolution. Though there's a touch of ugliness in his determination to let us know without seeming to that certain socialites with gentile names weren't born that way, "Radical Chic" is sometimes acute in its dramatization of this case. But theory cruelly limits the meaning to be found. The Panthers can't be much more than props in this drama, and the host's famous gaffe—when Cox denies resenting the affluence so visible around him, Bernstein blurts out, "Well, it makes *me* mad!"—can only enact muddled liberal fatuosity, not also a genuinely bewildered sense of impasse that might have some human resonance.

It of course plays into a satirist's hand to complain that he's unserious, but four books in six years have worn the sheer fun of Wolfe's game a bit thin. In *The Electric Kool-Aid Acid Test,* his best book, his mind and style responded complexly to Ken Kesey, a subject strong and aware enough to resist the habitual superiority that now finds blacks and society culturati easy meat. Reading me the invitation to review this book, the Western Union operator pronounced the title "Radical Chick," and I wish she'd been right—maybe Bernadine Dohrn or Kathie Wilkerson could give Tom Wolfe's art the strenuous workout it needs if it's to prosper.

*Here the problem was similar, though the texts I was working with were less considerable. "Reading" popular interests like professional sports was becoming an intellectual fashion even as I wrote, and I think it a legitimate interest. But as a sports fan I kept feeling that the main point got left out: the importance of not taking sports too seriously, of knowing, however sheepishly, that playing or watching games is not very good evidence that one is as responsible and grown up as one can bear to be. I had to argue, that is, both against not taking sports seriously at all and against taking them seriously in the wrong way, by not sufficiently respecting how differently they please and disturb from the way in which, for example, "high" art or politics can please or disturb.*

# *Thinking about Sports*
(1971)

> I've come to see that a football is one of the most dehumanizing experiences a person can face . . . the racism and fraud, the unbelievable brutality that affects mind as much as body. To me, it is no accident that Richard Nixon, the most repressive President in American history, is a football freak, and that the sport is rapidly becoming our version of bread and circuses.
>
> —Dave Meggysey,
> *Out of Their League*

> I believe that sport, all sport, is one of the few bits of glue that holds our society together, one of the few activities where young people can proceed along traditional avenues, where objectives are clear, where the desire to win is not only permissible but encouraged and, conversely, where a man can learn how to lose without being destroyed by the experience.
>
> —Spiro T. Agnew,
> in *Sports Illustrated,* June 21, 1971

> You can always be a teacher or a social worker when you've reached thirty-five.
>
> —Jim Bouton, *Ball Four*

*I*N politics, opposites guide, sustain, and even comfort each other, and it's no great surprise to find Dave Meggysey and Spiro Agnew agreeing on what "sport" means, though not on what it does to people. For them both, sport represents society as it is or (for Agnew) ought to be. Agnew might have written the scenario for Meggysey's career, the poor Hungarian boy finding social identity as a high school and college football star and going on to modest success as a professional linebacker; and Meggysey's decision to quit, just as some of the recognition and money he'd worked so hard for started coming in, was a deliberate rejection of the "system" Agnew finds sport upholding.

In theory, of course, they're right—any collective human activity within a society in some way reflects the political structures that exist there. Yet neither man says much about my own relation to sport. Though athletics may well be good for young people, morally as well as physically, I can't pretend that my character or patriotic sense now benefits much from playing or watching. I hate to lose, personally or vicariously; some of my meanest and socially least useful emotions are aroused by games, to say nothing of the time lost for work or decent sociability. As citizen, parent, and workman, I would be better off not liking sport at all. But while my life is a betrayal of what Agnew and my old P.E. teachers hoped for from me, it doesn't live up to Meggysey's terms either—being a football fan doesn't really seem to have made me a napalm fan, a racism fan, a law-and-order fan.

Meggysey's conversion to the counterculture began, he explains, when he seriously injured an opponent, but it's a longer step between physical fierceness and "racism and fraud" than he allows. Blocks and tackles as such aren't racist or fraudulent, and the gentler sports are no cleaner than football in these respects. Like other sports, football is racist because the players, coaches, and owners have the prejudices of their class and background; it is fraudulent, in the sense Meggysey intends, because the men who run it for profit are at best no more altruistic and socially responsive than most businessmen; it is violent and subjectively brutal because it is football.

*Out of Their League* records an admirable growth of political awareness and conscience in an unexpected place, but its metaphors are too easy. The trouble with Nixon isn't that he watches football but that he makes such an obvious and cheap political gesture of it, companionably winking to the Silent Majority while the Peace Freaks parade outside. (If only one could believe that he does like football, or anything else, innocently and directly, without the nervous eyes searching about for the camera as the No. 3 Smile clicks into position! If lawn bowling or ballet were as popular as football, he'd watch.) As it is, the resemblances of football to war, which polo, arm wrestling, and shuffle-board in their own ways also resemble, lure Meggysey into a neat and conclusive connection-making that's the mark of soft thinking. To see politics everywhere is one thing, probably a salutary thing on the whole, but to see it there at the expense of the particular and obvious qualities of the object observed—to treat experience merely as an allegory of one's political hopes or fears—is dangerous, impoverishing nonsense, all the more so for not being confined to ex-linebackers.

If Dave Meggysey is a political moralist, a True Believer with the enthusiastic flush of revelation still upon him, Jim Bouton is something else, something more recognizably in the American grain of sport and its myths. To be sure, *Ball Four* operates as anti-myth, with its grinning exposure of the boozing, pill-popping, and sexual silliness of baseball players, the stupidity and greed of coaches and front-office people. Bouton is the Thersites of our epic sport, but like Thersites he counts on our prior veneration of the epic values, and he himself figures as the debunker who is both partly right and, because of his own incapacity, somehow not to be trusted. Scandalous revelations about demi-gods like Mantle, Yastrzemski, Crosetti, Maglie, and Berra, even if true, mean less than they otherwise might in the mouth of a sore-armed knuckleballer, struggling through what turned out to be his last full season in the game.

Bouton himself, for all his incidental sympathy for hippies, protest, and racial justice, is no radical but a screwball, a comic, a show-off. If he'd been a little less smart and sophisticated and his arm had held up, he might even have entered the pantheon himself, as the latest in the great line of Rube Waddell, Bugs Raymond, Babe Herman, Dizzy Dean, and Bobo Newsom. Those nicknames of course cry out for William Empson to come and read them—the "country" eccentric with irrepressible natural gifts is a prime type in baseball legend, the sign, I suppose, of its popular, folkish origins and its proletarian appeal once urbanized. (Our other major sports were developed mainly by college boys or rich men in private clubs.) In our version of pastoral, the baseball player may properly be as much clown as hero. But they only called Bouton "Jim"—his ironies are too knowing to seem Empsonianly clownish, and his satire stumbles over our (and his) sense of his failing prowess, the essentially defensive malice that's overt in the title of his feeble, synthetic second book, *I'm Glad You Didn't Take It Personally*.

Bouton's indifference to what baseball "expresses" so long as it's amusing and pays well preserves him from sociopolitical pomposities, but he avoids hyper-seriousness only by accepting—so as to invert—the gossipy personalization most American sportswriting substitutes for the analysis of performance it's too ignorant to attempt. (Compare soccer reporting in many European newspapers or bullfight criticism in Spain.) What Mickey Mantle is Really Like has little to do with what one saw in his great years. While fantasy is deeply involved in looking at sports, even the most simple-minded fan doesn't merely idealize the players so as to identify with their virtuous skill. As with movie stars or politicians, their glamour is partly in our sense that they are privileged, that some naughtiness may even be necessary if their privacy is to be as rich and luxurious as we hope it is. We don't, after all, give them fame and money just to live the way *we* do.

An interest in sport undoubtedly involves an element of wish-fulfillment—as fans we're surely trying to sustain connection with childhood, after most other connections have worn pretty thin. But the fantasy enacted has its own terms, various and sometimes fairly complicated ones. Meggysey's equation of Nixon as football watcher with Nixon as Cold War Commissar is less interesting and plausible than, for example, William Phillips's idea ("A Season in the Stands," *Commentary*, July 1969) that for male intellectuals sport, especially football, offers a "respectable" form of the primitive aggressiveness ("violence, patriotism, manhood") that even thinking men remain secretly fascinated with. (I do think Phillips's emphasis on how team loyalties reflect attachment to one's own city or community is excessive, at least in American terms; John Lindsay may have picked up some votes from the Mets' winning the Series a few weeks before the 1969 election, but even in New York most serious fans are less innocent than that. Think by comparison of soccer fans in Italy, Latin America, or Britain, for whom winning or losing may be quite literally a matter of life or death.) Yet Phillips also shows the limitations of seeing sport as war by going on to talk, not like a natural man appeasing his blood-lust in Yankee Stadium, but like a would-be coach, for whom the display of force leads to professional assessments of particular players, plays, and strategies. For the serious spectator, who knows what he's watching, vicarious participation in the physical acts is subordinate to imagined *direction* of the whole intricate show, a kind of fantasy that's less embarrassing and more fun for grownups.

For the audience, even those who respond strongly to violence and competition, sport is a form of art. We can't simply project ourselves into the players—their experience is quite unimaginable verbally or imagistically—but we can feel something of what it would be like to manage and conduct it all, determine the tactics and deploy the personnel. If these are the terms of warfare, it's war refined and formalized into the mood of campaign maps and military histories; without actually *doing* anything one feels the intellectual and aesthetic consequences of effective choices among the means available. At this level of disinterest (for all its dangers), sport and war are indeed related, but only through their affinities with other arts, which give pleasure by allowing us imagined participation in the discovery and disposition of means that made the work, the performance, be just as it is.

Such a claim is pompous if it aims at dignifying sport by associating it with something better, art. To be worth the time of intelligent people sport doesn't need that kind of validation—as a fan, I can only sneer at someone who wants to turn a great football or basketball game into listening to Mozart or looking at Cézannes. Besides its obvious preciousness and confusion of realms, that impulse would spoil another powerful strain of fantasy in American sportswatching, one's feeling that it's a "classless" diversion whose appeal isn't restricted by how one has defined oneself in the terms of taste, background, occupation, or intelligence. (This may be peculiarly American, or at least colonial. In England and some Continental countries an attachment to a particular sport—cricket or tennis vs. soccer or cycling, Rugby Union vs. Rugby League, etc.—may well reflect class identity or pretensions thereto. But this is surely a historical phenomenon, not evidence that the formal or stylistic terms of a given sport have intrinsic social significance—compare the radically different class appeal and atmosphere of structurally similar games like baseball and cricket.) A baseball game isn't "classical," "popular," "folk," or "rock," it's just baseball, good or bad; though to think too much about it is to turn into Nixon, I do somehow suppose that by going to Madison Square Garden or turning on the TV I enlarge or submerge my social identity as I can't with most other kinds of art.

But the difficulty is in the word "art," with its lingering elitist resonances, not in any absurdity about attaching to sport some of the interest and value we attach to literature, music, painting, or drama. Those who are already comfortable with an idea of art that takes in good journalism, pop music, film, commercial design, advertising, and so forth, should have no trouble here. (I'm obliged to Richard Poirier's instructive view of popular art, as advanced in "Listening to the Beatles" and elsewhere in *The Performing Self*.) Serious—as opposed to ignorant, not to pleasurable and unpretentious—observation of sport is an exercise of imagination, a participation in a formal "life" outside the limiting predispositions of class and taste. And by allowing a fantasy-content to it I don't suggest that its effects are trivial or unsubstantial. In watching sport our powers of attention and affection are enlarged and made more generous by being attached to actions that are admirably beyond our own performing abilities.

No doubt the self as sports fan is narrower and more static than the selves other arts invite us to experience. If sport doesn't turn us all into bullies, sadists, and war-mongers, neither does it often lead to the very finest possibilities of feeling and judgment. (In fact it can lead to, or at least objectify, obsession and madness, as in Robert Coover's *The Universal Baseball Association* and Frederick Exley's *A Fan's Notes*.) But in watching it one learns to value a physical life that's also a form of intelligence, all the more impressive—at least to the clerkly and sedentary—for operating pre-verbally, pre-conceptually, in the trained coincidence of strength, neural quickness, instinct, memory, and will.

Easy metaphors for what athletes do are just silly. Consider what might, and shouldn't, be made of this remark by Jerry Kramer, the great offensive guard of the Packers:

> I must get some enjoyment out of the game, though I can't say what it is. It isn't just the body contact. . . . Body contact gives me only cuts and contusions, bruises and abrasions. I suppose I enjoy springing a back loose, making a good trap block, a good solid trap block, cutting down my man the way I'm supposed to.
>
> *(Instant Replay)*

In that last phrase Meggysey, and Agnew too, may hear the voice of Lt. Calley—like the soldier, the athlete enacts our subservience to social and political system, our substitution, for good or ill, of authority for our own humanity. But even Jim Bouton, in his struggling persistence while the rewards were dwindling down, knew that there was something in sport for which teaching and social work, or, as it turned out, TV sports reporting, could happily be postponed a little longer, something more than obeying "the system" which he himself never stopped thumbing his nose at. In "the way I'm supposed to" I hear not just Jerry Kramer's subservience to Vince Lombardi, though Lombardi was indeed an archetypal establishmentarian tyrant, but also his understanding that his own performance, to be worth the effort expended, had to be intelligible to himself and others, and that such intelligibility requires an idea of painfully difficult perfection that can't be named in words but is recognizable, when achieved, by players and knowing spectators alike.

American professional athletes do pay for their fame and fortune by being subjected to economic and personal dependency of a very demeaning kind. Few other grown men are told when to go to bed or given as little say in how to do their work; it's like being in the army or in prison, though the pay and hours are better and no one is there against his will. But the subjective plight of the athlete is considerably less painful, to him or to me, than that of migrant farm workers or the urban poor; even the black athlete, of whom more is demanded (usually for less money), makes out better in sport than he would in most other American occupations, and he's not often *more* militant, to say the least, than his brothers outside. To make sport directly represent American life is not a very good way of understanding what's wrong with that life.

The experience of Meggysey and Bouton does prove that thoughtful and sensitive people aren't apt to be very happy as professional athletes, though no doubt it helps if one is superlatively skilled and plays for a winning team. But for the onlookers, this too is an element in the imaginative meaning of sport. What the players do *should* have little relation to thought and sensitivity as we know and value them outside sport—it feels simpler and mysteriously better than that. If this is pastoral fantasy, with its intimations of inexpressible virtue in the physical life, of persisting connections with childhood innocence, of a democratic transcendence of the social and cultural self-definitions that ordinarily separate us from other kinds of people, it's still a necessary and beneficent mode of self-imagining, whose fantasies are at least less harmful than some of the things sport can be confused with. Neither Bouton's scoffing, Meggysey's moral outrage, nor Agnew's bland benedictions help me very much to think about sport, which can't tell us much about the present state of society but helps a little in understanding and better respecting our own desires.

*Charles Manson came as a shock to us all, though more of one, I argued, than he really should have been. As I thought about my own shock at the Tate–La Bianca murders and their lurid background as pictured by Ed Sanders in* The Family, *the details seemed to touch upon lots of other unpleasantness we'd been enduring for some time, to say nothing of things that were not in themselves unpleasant at all—the movies and the landscape and* mores *of the American West, where I had lived contentedly some years earlier. I'm still surprised that more hasn't been written about Manson and serial murderers generally, as explications of the American Scene in our times.*

# Manson Country
(1973)

> Nobody knew that the deserts of the West, the arid empty wild blind deserts, were producing again a new breed of men.
> —Norman Mailer,
> *An American Dream*, 1965

"*H*I. I'm Charlie Manson," he's supposed to have said when they found him hiding in the bathroom cupboard up above Death Valley. It took two more months, some so-so police work, and quite a lot of luck to find out who Charlie Manson really was, or at least enough of it to see him as a significant figure in the violent decade that brought him his vocation. But his significance is easier felt than defined; his career and style point toward some aspects of modern America that are harder to come to terms with than Manson himself.

Anyone who knows the American west even casually will hear in that "Hi" a familiar, conventional yet not insincere cordiality that presumably aims at making the most of the loneliness of being alive in the midst of monumental emptiness. The style was of course southern and mid-western first, but it makes more sense in the gas stations and roadside cafés of the Far West, where the imagination of remoteness gets such poignant assistance from the eye, from seeing so much of the space that isolates you. In that landscape you almost have to say "Hi" (or "Howdy," or "How"), since any human contact, even with cops, is somehow welcome there, because somehow surprising and stimulating; and the conventional sign at the other end of the encounter, "Come back, now," almost means the anxiety it affects. But the style conceals even as it expresses—in that space seclusion feels normal and right, nature itself seems to forbid too much curiosity about what other people are really up to. And since western space also permits continual movement without having to explain yourself and doesn't seem noticeably diminished by the introduction of a few dead and mutilated bodies here and there, it was a fine landscape for Charles Manson and his friends.

There's something familiar in this nightmare, then, something that temptingly gestures toward larger feelings about American style in a difficult time. The rather surprising paucity of writing about Manson—Ed Sanders's *The Family* is the first ambitious consideration of him—suggests that his meaning is only too obvious to anyone of tolerable sense and virtue. What can the hippie life, with its pointed inversions of decency and law, lead to if not degeneracy, madness, and such ultimate horror as group-murder for kicks? Of if, like Ed Sanders, you take a more pastoral view of the countercultural impulse, you can read Manson elegiacally, as sad evidence of what went wrong with the beautiful dream of an alternative *communitas* somewhere Out There. Sanders's implicit theme is carried by broad but unproven hints that Mansonism was not a self-generated corruption but a contamination from outside, through Manson's supposed connections with existing, establishment-fostered evil: organized crime, movieland drugs-and-port networks, a lurid underground of occultists and demonists who (for example) practice human sacrifice on remote California beaches, the assassination of Robert Kennedy, and most of the unsolved murders in Greater Los Angeles between 1967 and 1969. In a world like ours, no Eden is secure.

Once this sort of game gets going, of course, reason and the rules of evidence must stand aside:

> It is possible that the Process [a British-based cult of alleged Satanists] had a baleful influence on Sirhan Sirhan since Sirhan is known, in the spring of '68, to have frequented clubs in Hollywood in the same turf as the Process was proselytizing. Sirhan was very involved in occult pursuits. He has talked several times subsequent to Robert Kennedy's death about an occult group in London which he knew about and which he really wanted to go to London to see.
>
> There was one Process member named Lloyd who was working as a chef for one of the larger Los Angeles hotels, either the Ambassador or the Sheraton. . . . It is probably a coincidence that Sirhan seems to have visited a friend who worked in the kitchen of the Ambassador Hotel the day before he shot Senator Kennedy.

Sanders deserves the abuse he's received for this sort of thing, and it wasn't surprising to hear recently that he and his publishers have had to retract many of the book's allegations about the Process. And certainly such wool-gathering doesn't help serious thinking about Manson: if he is more than a loathesome figure of burgherly moral allegory, he's also more than a pawn in some pop-Gothic thriller about universal conspiracy against the light. Sanders's Manson is as far from where we really live as is the Manson of middle-American tongue clucking.

Yet an unselective and messy approach to Manson has its

virtues. If Sanders's theories are mostly hopeless, his material is rich and suggestive, helping one to see that if Manson's story doesn't "mean" much of anything it nevertheless may *express* quite a lot. For Sanders, Manson was a kind of radio set picking up what was in the air in a strange time, and if this notion is useless to the lawyer or the psychiatrist, it may yet take a magpie's taste for the extraneous detail, the rationally absurd analogy, to get Manson into some kind of focus.

Certainly, with Sanders, we do well to ignore what the psycho-historian would want to begin with, the usual stuff about childhood and adolescence. The Manson who matters isn't a case history but a cultural artifact, a man whose life was accidentally blessed, or rather cursed, with an opportunity to escape his personal history and be born again as someone he'd had no reason to hope he could be. In 1960 he entered prison, not for the first time, as a car-thief, pimp, and petty forger, one of those sleazy tinhorns from Appalachia or the Great Plains who drifted to California in droves in the thirties and forties and later; in 1967, with his old impulses and skills sophisticated by prison studies in hypnotism, Scientology, guitar playing, and Robert Heinlein novels, he emerged into a world he himself might have made to be his ideal theater if he'd had the wit, one whose style and outlook had during his absence become a slicker if less authentic version of his own. In Berkeley and the Haight and up and down the coast kids were talking and dressing and acting like him. While the creatures of this brave new world had hard drugs to teach him (on his first acid trip he apparently experienced his own crucifixion, but then so did others), he could offer them not only a fantastic psychic and sexual magnetism but also the old lag's expertise in how to get what you want without actually paying for it.

He had of course missed the theoretical point of their case, the passive rejection of family, society, political and military horror that was meant to be implicit in their enactments of love, brotherhood, psychic transcendence, the simple life. He just wanted to make it big in show biz as a rock musician and songwriter, and when that failed he was content for a while to use his weirdo charisma to make himself interesting to some rather alarming Hollywood fringe-types, camping at their houses, using their cars and credit cards, letting them take dirty movies of himself and his girls around their pools. Manson was really a fear-freak, as Sanders suggests; his thing was power, not love or pleasure, certainly not justice or social revolution, but his style was hard to distinguish from that of thousands of others whose intentions were better or at least more confused. Certainly the police, who saw a lot of him even in those days, took him for just another hippie or, at worst, an oddly small and scrawny specimen of the bike-gangers he sometimes consorted with.

By the time of the Tate–La Bianca murders and those less publicized ones the Family also committed, Manson had of course gone beyond his profitable exploitation of foolish or decadent swingers. Historical accident had released him from his original self, but Manson Redivivus was generating its own new history, which must have been getting to feel as marginal and frustrated and unfree as the old one. Only at this point does violence become an overt motif in the Manson story. None of his earlier difficulties with the law seem to have involved physical viciousness; he was more grifter than hood, described by a police psychiatrist in 1959 as "not [giving] the impression of being a mean individual" and by his parole officer a year later as "this weak, tricky youth." (There are interesting parallels in the early police reports on Hitler.) Yet the Manson of 1967–69 grew increasingly obsessed by at least the style of violence, putting on terrific shows of temper within his group and working out the elaborate mystique of torture and killing that led to all the murders.

From the Beatles' White Album he derived his obsession

with "Helter-Skelter," a vision of impending social apocalypse through a black revolution; he formulated elaborate plans of escape in dune buggies across the Mohave to Death Valley, where he and his people would hide out until the blacks were ready to hand over the world to him. The murders seem to have been, in part, exercises in loyalty and nerve for his followers—Manson himself apparently wasn't present at the Tate–La Bianca killings, much less an active participant. And here there's an intriguing parallel. Though Sanders estimates that Manson, who disdained contraception like any sexist male, copulated some three thousand times during the two and a half years of the major phase, only once did he get anyone pregnant. It seems to have worried him—happiness isn't a warm gun if your gun isn't loaded.

Whether collective and calculated or individual and impulsive, violence, I suppose, is an effort to escape a history that's felt as intolerable. In rejecting reason, argument, law, the structures of responsibility and affection that urge a withholding of force from others, the violent man destroys his socialized self and strikes out into an unknown territory that feels exhilaratingly like freedom, at least until he gets there and begins (perhaps) to be ashamed or apprehensive. For Manson, I imagine, the mystique of violence was in effect a mode of self-recreation. Twice-born through cultural accident but aware that his second life was petering out, he may dimly have sensed that through violence yet another new self might come to be. Murder offered at least the illusion of power, in the form of an anonymous publicity to make up for the rock-star's fame he'd failed to achieve. And murder would objectify adequately the awe and fear that his followers, psychic cripples and unfinished adolescents as they were, needed so badly to invest in someone.

At this point, or maybe well before it, we do better to turn away from Manson himself. If his career makes an appalling kind of psychological and political sense, it remains a trivial and, in its own terms, uninstructive one. But as his story leads away from him and toward the world we must after all share with him, his effort to make myth of his own life, by living out a style adequate to the terms of America in the sixties, has considerable interest.

One is struck, first of all, by how easy it was for him to live. Where good citizens have to worry about money and practical arrangements, the acquisitive society, with its necessary devotion to waste, virtually thrusts its excess benefits upon shiftless but shifty non-producers like Charlie Manson. Where to spend a night, or several weeks?—the Los Angeles basin is full of comfortable or luxurious domiciles whose owners think nothing of being crashed by a dozen or two homeless creeps. (If they tire of you, they don't call the police but move out themselves, as some of Manson's hosts and hostesses did.) People who lack cash-money may have credit cards, even the waifs and runaways who clustered around Manson, and, apparently with the thought that a lost child isn't really lost if the bills keep coming in, their parents often paid up indefinitely. You can always steal a car, obviously, but if like Manson you hobnob with prosperous yet Bohemian creative people like the Beach Boys, there are apt to be sports cars, jeeps, or Rolls-Royces available for long-term loans. (The owner may, however, have to go out to Death Valley and pay some repair bills when he wants his wheels back.) Legitimate money can always be picked up hustling rich women, selling a little dope, or turning out some of your girls around the Sunset Strip; but the proceeds can be reserved for important capital expenditures like guns and bail bonds, since there are garbage cans full of only slightly-worn produce to be had behind any of the better supermarkets. And of course, unlike the ordinary burgher, for whom travel is an event that requires money, planning, and anxiety, you can go anywhere anytime and stay as long as you like.

If you have drugs and sex and a distinctive philosophy of

life to offer, that is, you will find America today as hospitable as Manson did. And when, as occasionally will happen, someone finds your fatal charm resistible and calls the cops, he will find that as a police state the U.S. is an awful flop. Before and after the murders Manson was continually being arrested for narcotics offenses, fraud, traffic violations, auto theft, statutory rape, and so on; yet the charges were always dropped, even though he was on parole from a federal prison. He was finally connected with the Tate–La Bianca affair only because an eleven-year-old boy found a gun in his backyard and then had his father remind the police about it months later, when it had completely slipped their minds.

But if Manson's story doesn't quite jibe with the old Cagney films where your iron-eyed parole officer followed you around hoping you'd spit on the sidewalk, still the movies loom large in the Manson story. One can't of course live in Southern California at all without feeling Hollywood as an essential part of the ambiance. It's just *there,* and too much shouldn't be made of the appearance of Will Rogers State Park and Leo Carrillo Beach in the Manson mise en scène. But as accumulated by Ed Sanders's fan-mag curiosity, meaningless movie-lore begins to seem a necessary dimension of the story. Manson came out of prison with a contact at Universal Studios, hoping to promote it into a career in recording and maybe even films; when he began, like Ken Kesey, to transport his people around in an old school bus, they posed as a traveling movie crew, on the reasonable assumption that people will accept any kind of behavior if it has to do with Hollywood. Robert Beausoleil, his most effective male associate and the first of the group to be charged with murder, was at least nominally a professional actor, who had worked in Kenneth Anger films and skin-flicks. Various children of Hollywood personages had some marginal contact with the family, and the house in which Sharon Tate and her friends were killed had been visited by Manson before, while it was occupied by Doris Day's son, whom Manson apparently knew fairly well. (Jay Sebring, one of the victims, himself lived in Jean Harlow's old place.) The Spahn Ranch, the family's Los Angeles headquarters, was an old-time movie location (once owned by William S. Hart), which was still occasionally used for low-budget westerns, beaver films, and Marlboro Country commercials. The family itself was hooked on making home movies, pornographic and otherwise, and Sanders says that they took a stolen NBC-TV camera along to record their last retreat to Death Valley, where, at a godforsaken distance from any paved road or permanent habitation, they made their headquarters near an abandoned mine owned by (who else?) Warner Brothers.

Publicity, the expedient narcissism that makes Hollywood go, was Manson's medium of self-imagination long before the case broke and he turned up so sensationally on *our* home screens. If he thought himself divine, Manson Son of Man, it was in the person of Jesus Christ, Superstar; if he was the devil, he played it with the lurid flourishes of a zonked-out stage Mephisto. Or ("Hi. I'm Charlie Manson") he could be just plain Gary Cooper, with the easy grace of the simple man with something in reserve. All of Manson's roles in fact derive from us, from cultural materials we created and happily consumed long before there was a Manson to act out their worst possibilities. Movieland was the right arena for him, remembering that Movieland isn't just posh poolside Beverly Hills and groovy Malibu beach pads but also the strange and empty moonscape all around, that western American space that needs filling with *something*, if only with celluloid dreams of Lawrence's "essential American soul," the hard, integral, unsocial and yet magnetic Deerslayer, the "isolate, almost selfless, stoic enduring man, who lives by death, by killing, but is pure white."

In Lawrence's terms, obviously, Manson represents that soul in disintegration even more clearly than do some other possible contemporary instances. With the style of the counterculture as cover, from both the law and some of his more naïve followers, he was yet an essentially conventional and undisruptive type, feeling out the weak spots in our social fabric, not to expose and destroy but to creep inside and get his share. He reminds us, if we need reminding, that crime may not represent resistance to an established order but an expression of that order's values in extremis. Just how, subjectively, exploitive aggression turns into suicidal destructive madness is as mysterious at the personal level as at the public and political, but Manson and Calley have some representational value in common, and beyond them stand Johnson and McNamara, Nixon and Kissinger, and most of the rest of us.

At any rate, Manson's final flight to the Mohave was mythically right. The desert is both the quintessence of American space, with its promise of freedom, and also the terrible end of that promise, littered with worn-out cars, refrigerators, aircraft, and general junk, already tinged with the L.A. smog from 200 miles away. It looks rather like Vietnam, I suppose, or like the Apollo landing sites, where all that useless equipment sits forever. (Would Aldrin and Armstrong have been quite so stirring if the moon weren't so evidently a John Wayne set?) The desert's few people, outside the SAC bases and ordnance proving-grounds, are mainly prospectors and miners, still hopefully seeking the big bonanza of gold, silver, or tungsten, the "Grand Glory Hole" that was somehow missed in the prosperous days when the ghost towns were lively and the mines productive, before our national greed had so desperately depleted the earth. (Manson's mad search for "The Hole" of Hopi legend, the hidden entrance to an underworld of bliss and security somewhere beneath Death Valley, is a curious and touching parallel.) The desert is a junkheap, a graveyard for nature and technology wedded in mutual death. It was the right place for Charlie Manson, whose dreadful story yet reflects a bewildered desire saner and better people, here and now, may also feel.

The California Supreme Court abolished the death penalty in time to spare him and his poor, dumb, stupefied girls, and that seems all right. We can't rid ourselves of what he signifies by killing him. But like others who have seen and felt more than they can understand, he may well want to die, and if by any chance the chair in the gas chamber at San Quentin faces eastward, it would have made some sense to think of him sitting there, like Deerslayer, at the end.

*Feminist criticism and theory have come a long way since I wrote about these novels by women, but I still think—though without wanting to argue about it—that the best goal is not some segregation of writings on the basis of gender but a literature in which "female" and "male" give us mutually instructive perspectives on what is finally, I hope, just "human." But of course I understand that men have written most of the history, literary and otherwise, and that a lot of revision has to be done.*

# *Women's Fiction*
(1974)

"Women's fiction" used to mean the soft and sticky fantasies of love and domestic power out of which Richardson invented the novel and which Joyce raised to excruciating clarity in the person of poor Gerty MacDowell. I don't think women should be particularly embarrassed about this—the hard and lumpy stuff of "men's fiction," with *its* fantasies of love and power, is certainly no more distinguished, and the great novelists, male or female, are more like Gerty MacDowell than James Bond or Tarzan. But the tradition I'm thinking about obviously reflects a social, political, and sexual subordination of women that's no longer much of a secret, and I don't wonder that women writers are looking for other ways of doing things.

Yet feminine self-consciousness remains in an undeservedly difficult situation. Good writing comes out of an engagement with something that one knows, while trying not to give the impression that it's all one knows. Our cultural arrangements, however challenged these days, still ensure that most intelligent and morally curious women are allowed only a relatively small range of opportunities for experience, and hence for writing fiction about how women live.

This limiting of possibilities struck me painfully when I

noticed that both Marge Piercy and Eleanor Bergstein, who don't otherwise seem to have much in common besides being writers and women, have put episodes in their recent novels that are strikingly similar. One of their heroines (each book has two), a girl who's big and sexy and Jewish and in or just out of college, relinquishes her virginity after being picked up in the Museum of Modern Art by what turns out to be Mr. Wrong (in each case a writer), who carries her up to his place for a splendid lay. No doubt that stimulating institution does preside over such liaisons, and the irony of first love being a (fallible) form of aesthetic education works well enough in both books; but "women's fiction" of the old school seems somehow close by, and it's sad that a trivial coincidence should seem to say so much about what even tough and sophisticated women writers have to work with.

One way of dealing with such limitations, of course, is to accept them and give them the imaginative works, as Rhoda Lerman does in *Call Me Ishtar*. Here the small and seemingly hopeless details of Middle American housewifery get infused with wild strains of myth, as the archetypal mother—call her Ishtar or Astarte or Aphrodite or Arianrhod or whatever else Robert Graves or Norman O. Brown may suggest—descends into the fallen world of rational male order somewhere around Syracuse, New York, in the incarnate form of a sexy, Jewish (see above) homemaker:

> My nipples are antennas, grossly exaggerated in the curved reflection of the Sunbeam toaster. They will understand when the toast should pop and will warn me before it burns. Robert, watching the stainless steel nipples, forgets that his juice is freshly squeezed and swallows the pulpy clots, coughing them into his

napkin. I smile secretly. He has not yet put down his paper. He is now reading the financial section. Before while I spoke to him of Cupcakes and factories and an entire civilization living on the chocolate and mandrake roots of my Hostess Cupcakes, and like happiness, being sold on every street corner of America, of the world and the mothers of the boys operating the factories while Robert sits far above them all, overseeing and designing new ovens and machines and checking quality control, he suddenly laughed between my words. He was reading Dagwood Bumstead. I continued to spin my dreams of edible records, of spruce beer and pears and happiness and wealth enough for the boys' contentment and his own peace, of peace between man and woman, of wholeness for everyone and of a connection again to the powers of heaven. He laughed. But what can I expect of him. He went to the bookstore to buy a copy of *Intelligent Life in the Universe* and when he arrived, forgot the title.

I don't know whether it's Ishtar or Lerman who here forgets that the title of that comic strip is really "Blondie," but it's amusing enough to watch Dagwood Bumstead reading Dagwood Bumstead oblivious to a wife who has feathers instead of pubic hair.

Some of the fun, however, seems pretty special and labored. The Hostess Cupcake business keeps coming up, as Ishtar goes about putting her own special recipe for them (Twinkies too) into mass production, and this remains baffling until she spells it out to the youthful audience at a rock show:

"Listen to their tales of original sin. The church hangs you up and shakes you down as they did me from the

> Tree of Life, for I am the apple and it is I that must be eaten for knowledge and joy. But they rip you off too. Sign nothing. Promise nothing. Don't sell your soul for their redemption. You have no sin. Remember the Hostess. Jesus is bad hash. Partake of me."

There are too many such tricks in Lerman's way of connecting heaven and earth to the detriment of unalterable law, man-style. Ishtar's housewife-self is married to Robert, a plastics manufacturer whose secret name, she divines, is Moses, one of her old enemies; and this joke, like others, gets played out in endless variations, from driving on the Robert Moses Power Access Highway on page one to Ishtar's farewell to "my ex-Chairman of Parks and Paradise" at the end.

Sometimes one enjoys the ingenuities, as when Ishtar's fond memory of her recreation of the world after the Deluge, coupling with Noah on Ararat to the music of "By the Time I Get to Phoenix," leads many pages later to:

> Luck, who not only is a Lady, but is from the same source word as Logos, lucifer and means wisdom, light, power, might bring me a Phoenix flapping against my Spanish ceiling beams. Phoenix, by the way, originates from the same source as Venus, Penis, Phoenicia, and Phoenicia is the place where circumcision was first, according to your histories, practiced in my honor.

But there's something rather desperate about the continual invocation of the myth of primal feminine power. If Lerman's handling of it is mostly pretty goodnatured and often quite funny, still it keeps pushing the book up against a seriousness that it can't quite accommodate:

> The Angel of Death, the Whore of Babylon, the Mother of the World, we must be all these things, Claire, all at once. That woman you have on your coins with the balanced scales? She is not justice. She is woman balancing her roles. Standing on one foot, blindfolded. Half queen, half whore, half goddess, half kitchen help. "Cunt, my dear fornicating child," I tell Claire as we drive to Rochester, with Grace and her friend behind us in their aprons under their pastel mink-collared coats and their Dynel wigs.
>
> "*Cunt, my sweet child, is from the Sumerian word cunnus, It means Burden. It is not something to be treated lightly....*"

But for Lerman it is not something to be treated heavily, either; big guns roll up only to fire off cupcakes, the kidder and the suffragette keep elbowing each other aside.

*Call Me Ishtar* reflects a sense of what could fairly be called oppression, a sense Lerman obviously shares with many other women. But I think that women face a special difficulty in expressing this sense, one that black writers, for example, may not face. Lerman's book reminds me interestingly of Ishmael Reed's *Mumbo Jumbo*, which also relates the culture of an oppressed group to a body of lore drawn from mythography and comparative religion and in which the myths invoked unexpectedly make more sense than the satiric occasion requires. But if women are an oppressed group, they are not an oppressed *minority* group; in practical terms, at least, they have less to gain and more to lose than blacks do, and a sense of qualified oppression can create imaginative uneasiness. Where Reed uses his mythic materials with a fine, incisive arrogance, Lerman seems a little nervous. Where Reed doesn't bother to discriminate, Lerman seems unsure about what's "serious" and what isn't, over-anxious to make something, preferably something dignifying, of the housewife's lot.

Virginia Woolf once remarked that "when a woman speaks to women she should have something very unpleasant up her sleeve." Rhoda Lerman finally doesn't, I think, but Marge Piercy makes up for her. Though she contributes to *Call Me Ishtar* an approving dust-jacket blurb about "the emergence of a conscious and fully developed women's culture," Piercy has a harder message for women, and for men too. *Small Changes* begins in Lerman country, with the marriage in Syracuse of Beth, a blue-collar child vaguely yearning for something more than she has known, to Jim, a bundle of sexist fixations on sports, cars, TV, home cooking, and getting children; it's a grindingly circumstantial demonstration that the task for women isn't to make something of the domestic life but to discredit and escape it.

Beth, uneducated but capable of serious self-imaginings, runs away to Boston, gets a secretarial job at M.I.T., and gingerly explores the marginal area between the graduate-student culture and the bohemia of street life; gradually she learns that what she wants—separateness, the right to determine her own desires, a room of one's own—is as hard to find there as it was back home. Her life gets entangled with that of Miriam, who looks more like a fictional winner—she's a "big flamboyant" girl, sensual, out-going, brilliant at computer science, seemingly liberated to start with. But Miriam can't stop equating "reality" with being wanted by a man; she moves through intense and wearing relationships with two sexually challenging but humanly closed-in Vietnam veterans (who, Piercy suggests, have a subconscious homosexual thing for each other), emerging into a relatively conventional suburban marriage to a young scientist whose good nature is weaker than his male chauvinism; at the end he is drifting into an affair with his secretary while Miriam copes with the kids and enters psychotherapy. And, as Miriam goes under, Beth breaks out into commune life, lesbianism, and political resistance, achieving a tentative but rewarding security living in Cleveland under an assumed name with her dancer-organizer friend and the latter's children.

None of this is much fun to follow, partly because Piercy's people lead hard and unhappy lives, which is fair enough, but partly because she's determined to have her characters articulate their every motive in long, serious, searching talks about themselves and their problems:

> "I don't want to be poor, if the truth be known. I want to live comfortably. I'm tired of the half-life of a student. I want to be able to help my friends when they need help. I want to buy interesting clothes. I'm sick of eating in greasy spoons. I don't want a lot of money, Allegra, really. I just want a decent living. I want the things that make life pleasant. When I bought that reconditioned air conditioner for fifty dollars, do you know what a change that made in my life? This room gets hot in the summer, believe me, right up under the roof. I had enough hard times growing up."

This is Miriam, and the passage is diagrammatically right— her wants, none of them unreasonable alone, yet point toward the compromise with social comforts that finally undoes her. But the voice is too flat and sketchy, the mind behind it incompletely imagined; conversation in the book is a vehicle for debate about "life," not the dramatic record of conflicting feelings; everyone listens and replies to everyone else, people always say what they mean, and I suppose that Piercy would think it illegitimate authorial intrusion to allow into such a passage the little inadvertent, only partly conscious, nearly irrelevant private quirks of speech that could have turned it into a Chekhovian aria of self-revelation.

The virtue of Piercy's method is that it's consistently compassionate and fair to the novel's people, all of whom get room to work out their own terms for themselves. But the method also suggests a suspicion of words, a fear that most of what really matters will get messed up if anything more than the simplest operations of language (which are also the longest and most tedious) are performed. Phil, Miriam's first love, embittered by public and private disaster, turns from poetry to furniture making, with the author's apparent blessing, and Miriam herself comes as close as she ever gets to an adequate occupation when she and Phil set up as bakers of homemade bread for the local trade. Though Piercy never overtly endorses this familiar and sadly innocent insistence that life can be simpler and better than our ways of describing it, the book adds up to something close to endorsement.

The practical equivalent to a wordless life would I suppose be a life wholly outside the deceptive complications of the normative social, political and familial vocabularies, some "countercultural" existence of the sort that Miriam loses and Beth precariously finds; only there can women, and men too, achieve an authentic selfhood. Perhaps so; but the idea has its serious difficulties, and Piercy's nominal withholding of judgment doesn't convince me that the book has considered these with enough skepticism. Here is Beth thinking about her life in a New Hampshire commune:

> The men there were the first men Beth had been real friends with. Everyone in that house had been through

a year and a half of fighting their old attitudes and consciously trying to play equal and looser roles. Men who had been involved in such a struggle were different in obvious and subtle ways. They had different manners and different anxieties. In gross ways the house was unlike other communes: the men cooked too and the women also chopped wood and the men took care of the children and the women climbed up on ladders and worked side by side repairing the roof. One of the men, Alan, did needlepoint for pleasure. He was also accurate with a rifle.

The tone of rather naïve surprise is undoubtedly Beth's alone, but at some level Piercy obviously shares her pleasure in the image of a life in which people are emerging from culturally-imposed sexual roles. I can share that pleasure myself, but only while remembering that images aren't literal cases and wishing that this particular one weren't so tidy, that Alan was in fact a bad shot with a rifle, that more weight could be given to "consciously trying to play." Marge Piercy is an admirably serious writer, but her exploration and analysis of "roles" may lead to the erosion of "character" and a consequent obscuring of the possibilities of freedom her characters so urgently pursue. *Small Changes* tends to reduce its people to the social and political terms they are meant to enact; and while this, it could be argued, is a necessary stage in the revolution of consciousness the book hopes to contribute to, it seems in the short run at least an ambiguous artistic and human achievement.

Where Lerman and Piercy are in some sense (not a derogatory one) provincial novelists, both geographically and culturally, Eleanor Bergstein is visibly a cosmopolitan one. She assumes a common fund of experience and outlook in her readers, male or female, a sense of contemporary life founded on a moral commitment to politics and a sophisticated relation to informational media, a readiness for certain kinds of jokes, for example, that I myself am only too ready for:

> When she started to feel better she bought a lavender tweed coat with frog closings, and was taken around the city [Hong Kong] by the guide who had taken around Liz Taylor and Mike Todd. "She's beautiful," he said, "and he say to me 'Tommy you smaht boy I want you Carifoonia' and she say 'what is this clap?' and he say 'shut up you dum blawd' and she cly."

I'm not particularly anxious to examine my amusement at this, which must draw upon racial condescensions and the mixture of desire and malice any media-voyeur feels; but Bergstein knows that readers like me are out there ready to take such bait, and she plays us with considerable skill.

*Advancing Paul Newman* looks back from the Eugene McCarthy campaign of 1968 to the lives of Ila Rappaport and Kitsy Frank, who met as college girls in Europe in the summer of 1959 and remained best friends through the following decade. The book's design is elaborately cinematic, cutting regularly between campaign incidents and earlier events in the girls' lives, so that the past moves toward us even as the narrative present advances more slowly, with the assassination of Robert Kennedy and the death of Kitsy's husband in Vietnam marking the eventual coinciding of the two time tracks. The ingenuity of this feels rather mechanical for a while, but gradually one accepts it as a metaphor for the experience of history the novel intends. We do remember our lives as if they were old movies, and it can be shocking to discover, as do Ila and Kitsy, that ourselves watching the movie is part of the movie, that we remember not from outside our lives but from inside them, where things still are happening that we will only be able to "remember" in the future.

And the structure draws upon an understanding that we live in and through media more largely than it's altogether comfortable to recognize. The girls enter the adult world as bright college girls (and boys) used to do frequently, working at a succession of jobs in publishing, educational television, film agencies, promotion of various sorts. The book's catchy title—Ila and Kitsy work with an advance team for McCarthy's appearances in California that for a memorable few days includes Paul Newman himself—puts the irony forward. The actor is more vividly and compellingly real than the politician who's nominally the center of it all. History itself is a promotion, a media event, so that for most of us the sixties are framed between seeing (say) the killing of Lee Harvey Oswald or the Beatles' first performance on the Ed Sullivan Show and Johnson's abdication speech. "What happened" is reduced to recalling where we were and how we felt when a given newness, usually horrifying, appeared on the tube.

As public and private events blur together and become almost indistinguishable from invented commercial-aesthetic events, it gets very hard to be oneself. Ila and Kitsy first made connection by discovering that they liked and could quote from the same World War II movies (they'd of course missed the war itself); and when Kitsy finally has to grieve for her dead husband she's hard put to it to find an adequately personal way:

> I won't think you're brave I won't think you're smart I'll hate you I'll scream fool fool—would he have fought for himself? got killed in three days—hero starr louis starr mrs starr—cheering—leader—music swells, oh louis—grenade in a ditch gonna kill

gooks—john wayne idiot arching back like paul muni in norway bleeding like gone with the wind anatole kuragin without a leg john lennon red-crotched and comforting woman's face seamed with tenderness comes over the hill—it'll be all right dear it'll be all right.

This difficulty is hardly peculiar to women, and the impressive thing about *Advancing Paul Newman* is that Bergstein, while giving us Ila and Kitsy's experience as the experience of particular women (here Kitsy confusedly trying to identify with a feminine image from a decidedly masculine movie, *How I Won the War*), also transcends sexual categories. Ila and Kitsy *are* women, just as they are privileged, well-educated, upper-middle class, Jewish, New Yorkers; but in presenting their histories Bergstein shows all of us how much we've had to endure and how little of ourselves we've had available for the task.

It's a curious though hardly decisive fact that all three of these novels have a dual protagonist—in Lerman, Ishtar's double identity as housewife and deity, in Piercy and Bergstein literally two heroines whose fates are different. Maybe this schizoid habit marks a fairly early stage in the emergence of a new feminine consciousness, as if women writers were not quite ready to project their sense of their condition into a single, unequivocal fictional counterpart who could risk failure, or for that matter success, without having a stand-by self ready to bear some of the other possibilities. "Woman balancing her roles," as Lerman says, is a figure of affecting difficulty, to be watched with sympathy and hope. (Can a man say that without sounding patronizing?) But in the long run, I think the goal may not be a new "women's fiction" as such but a fiction that can represent the lives of women as part of the general life of people. This would require women writers to write as well about *men* as George Eliot or (at her best) Virginia Woolf did, as well as a few men writers like Richardson and James and (at his best) Lawrence have written about women. However imperative it now is for women to learn to understand, accept, and trust their identities as women, this (as they surely know too) will get them only half-way along the journey, though that's at least as far as men have got, and with a head start.

*I first read Dashiell Hammett when I was quite young—evidence, perhaps, that no lasting harm need be done by entrusting "unsuitable" books to children—and Raymond Chandler in my teens. Ross Macdonald came later, both in real time and in my reading, and I felt right away that he wasn't quite a match for his predecessors. But the Lew Archer novels intrigued me even so, no doubt in part because I'd lived for eight years in Southern California and recognized Archer's ambiance. Writing this piece gave me an opportunity to think about my own addiction—I really* had *read all the Archer books several times—and to weigh its pleasures against those of a really good novel which drew on but remade an interesting popular genre.*

# *Tough Guys*
(1976)

*I*T'S hard for sophisticated people to like something simple without overrating it, as the case of Ross Macdonald shows. Like those of his masters, Dashiell Hammett and Raymond Chandler, Macdonald's "tough" detective stories have been getting considerable attention and praise from serious readers, and, though I've read all twenty of the Lew Archer novels, most of them more than once, I'd recommend more caution in judging them. Even an addict can see that they are formulistic, unevenly written, and less than profound as social and psychological commentary. Yet the genre itself still pleases, and if a good and imaginative thriller like Paul Theroux's *The Family Arsenal* puts a piece of routine tough stuff like Macdonald's *The Blue Hammer* in its place as literature, it's clear that they have something important in common.

Under his real name, Kenneth Millar, Macdonald began in the 1940s as a writer of what now seem embarrassing melodramas about Axis espionage or the adventures of returning service men. The invention of Lew Archer in 1949 led to a better subject, the ironies of contemporary, affluent life in California, an apparently new and free world in which the privileged and the deprived could yet be shown, through Archer's investigations, to have common and appalling roots in the past. But World War II remains the source of trouble in many of the Archer books. *The Blue Hammer* hinges upon a murder in 1943, when a soldier home on leave killed his half-brother in the Arizona desert and took over his name, his wife, and his (undeserved) reputation as a promising young artist; and many of the other novels also reach back to that dark time when American men and women, dislocated from familiar identities and sound commitments, took the fatal step into error whose consequences have dogged them ever since. I suspect that Macdonald would not be displeased, or surprised, by a comparison to the Greek tragedians on Troy.

Archer himself is a resolutely neutral, even neuter, figure. He lives modestly and alone, seldom has much money, does without extra-professional friends or interests. (He claims to know nothing of arts or letters, for example, though Macdonald, who does know about them, sometimes forgets this). His personal reticence still permits glimpses of an unsettled childhood on the West Coast, service with the Long Beach police in the thirties, a stint with Intelligence during the war, a painful divorce. He is modern man reduced almost to pure function, the solving of mysteries, though a moralizing softness quivers within his hard-boiled shell.

You know where you stand with Archer, that is, and if he's less interesting than Chandler's Marlowe or the various heroes of Hammett, no great loss is incurred; one of the pleasures of the genre is its alluring suggestion that actions matter more than agents, that why means less than how. An Archer story, properly, subordinates "character" to the details of the problem at hand. Whatever the immediate crime—murder, theft, a missing person—a history of worse crimes lies concealed within it. In *The Blue Hammer* Archer must work backward from a stolen painting to the disappearance of its painter twenty-five years ago, and behind *that* event, it gradually emerges, lies a sequence of other events which began with an illegitimate birth sometime before 1920. New crimes point back to old ones, names are changed to protect the guilty, and a complex but (for Macdonald) surprisingly guessable series of revelations establishes that everyone is everyone else's parent, child, or sibling.

Macdonald has been shaping this plot into baroque extravagance through a quarter-century of Archer stories. The ingredients are simple if rather Calvinistic: crime is the legacy young and relatively innocent people must accept from the past; money and status are found to be tainted by the acquisitive process; the emergence of true history leaves assumed history in wreckage. A prosperous but sterile culture, for which California will do as an image, discovers its hidden sources. And that discovery, while shattering to the characters, becomes oddly gratifying to the reader. The passions that have created the present are, when revealed, recognizably human in their energies, somehow preferable, for all their wasteful folly, to the dead West Coast reality which Archer, his employers, and his antagonists must now inhabit. The reader can assume, that is, that a seemingly accidental and banal world makes sense, if only the negative sense of moral irony. Whether or not you believe it of California or other places, it's somehow reassuring to hear that cultural emptiness hasn't just happened, for no good reason.

Macdonald's basic plot makes literal the assumption of any mystery story, secular or theological: every crime conceals a moral history that can be reconstructed and understood. Apart from perfunctory questions of "motive," this history is usually a brief one—a few days, hours, even minutes within which someone unknown did something unpleasant to the victim—and Macdonald's extension of it into a remote past is rather grand and Miltonic. But otherwise his fictional resources seem limited: his characters are sketchy, their misdeeds uninventive, Archer's moral sense, inside his toughness, conventional and sedate.

Nor, compared with Chandler's talent for imagery or Hammett's for atmosphere, can Macdonald's writing claim much interest. *The Blue Hammer*, like most of the later Archer books, begins with a glimpse of western landscape that's somehow portentous:

> I drove up to the house on a private road that widened at the summit into a parking apron. When I got out of my car I could look back over the city and see the towers of the mission and the courthouse half submerged in smog. The channel lay on the other side of the ridge, partly enclosed by its broken girdle of islands.

This quickly attributes to Archer's clients the privilege that can command private roads and fine vistas, and, like the mountaintop converted to parking lot, the smog that impinges on the architecture of divine and human order hints broadly at the larger social malaise. But the third sentence is mere laziness. That "broken girdle" of islands sounds too literary for Archer, who has surely not read "Dover Beach" or "To Marguerite" lately, and a natural fact is asked to mean more than it can—all islands are disconnected, and if the girdle were unbroken the channel would I suppose be a lake.

A glance at the opening of *The Family Arsenal* shows how much more can be done with words. As it happens, Theroux also begins with an elevated view of an ordinarily smoggy city:

> Seated on a cushion at the upstairs window of the tall house, Hood raised the cigarette to the sun and saw that it was half full of the opium mixture. Filling it was pleasurable, like the willful care of delaying for love: to taste confidence. He winked and sighted with it, as if studying violence from afar, to take aim. He had a marksman's princely squint and the dark furious face of an Apache; but he was only finding his landmarks with the unfinished cigarette.
>
> He moved it slightly to the left and covered a

church steeple on the next road. In the slow fire of the late afternoon the tall granite spire had the look of an old dagger. Then to the right, past the far-off bulb of the Post Office Tower, a matchstick in metal; past a row of riverside warehouses the sun had gutted, and more burnt spires, and the dome of St. Paul's—blue and simple as a bucket at this distance. Drawing the cigarette down he measured a narrow slice of the river between two brick buildings charred by shadow: part of a wharf, the gas works, the power station pouring a muscle of smoke into the sky, a crane poised dangerously like an ember about to snap, housetops shedding flames. . . .

This scene powerfully reflects the observer's situation: Hood is on the verge of joining the IRA Provos in their campaign against a London he envisions as already burning. But his involvement is as yet only theoretical—the city, like the cigarette, is still unlit. If he's a marksman taking aim, he relishes the gap between thought and deed, and he's also represented as a kind of painter, an artist of his own intentions measuring the scene as if the cigarette were a brush, before blocking in his composition.

Expelled from the American consular service in Vietnam for slugging a local politico who'd spoken contemptuously of his own people, Valentine Hood ("tender tough guy," as it were) brings a dislike of unearned privilege and an instinct for violence to London, where he falls in with petty terrorists—a teenage bomb-maker and his bird, who's blown up a locker at Euston Station, and a well-born older woman, Mayo, who's stolen a minor Flemish painting to hold for ransom. They all live together in South London, a parody-family which yet has its warmth and affection, while Hood tries to make contact with the Provo inner circle and a political violence he can take more seriously.

Hood is a very rough customer indeed. He beats to death Ron Weech, a petty crook whom he hardly knows, just because the man is a bully and a braggart. Later he booby-traps a cache of stolen arms to get even with some toughs who've abused his new girlfriend, Weech's widow, blowing them up (along with poor Mayo) without a sign of remorse. A conventional thriller couldn't tolerate his violence, both because it's so severely amoral and because it's partly a device of conscious theater, a mimicry of (for example) the tough talk which writers like Macdonald ask us to take straight:

> Mayo lowered her voice. "There's a problem, Val. They want to talk to you. They think you can help them."
> "I used to think that."
> "Oh, God, don't tell me you're getting cold feet!"
> "Cold feet," said Hood, sneering. "Wise up, sister."
> "I knew it. As soon as things started to go your way you'd begin your consul act—the big, cool, noncommital thing."
> "I'll play it by ear."
> "They're coming tonight."
> "I might be out tonight."
> "I told them they could count on you."
> "They can count on me tomorrow. I've got other plans."

Even Lew Archer couldn't say "Wise up, sister" without blushing, but Theroux uses such clichés to suggest a taste for put-on and self-mockery that makes Hood seem all the more dangerous.

Hood's sense of the story he's part of is ambivalent in other ways as well. Though his professional disgrace and his attraction to terrorism seem to signify a sense of justice, his crimes are clearly nonpolitical, impulsive, gratuitous. The closer he gets to the Provos and their fashionable sympathizers, the more he despises their substitution of ideological play-acting for the efficient violence he yearns for. Theater is in fact the chosen medium of such people as Araba Nightwing, the radical actress whose gift for disguise the IRA exploits but whose own group, the Purple League, is finally reduced to disrupting Equity meetings, and Lady Arrow, the rich, bisexual "collector" of violent people and their emotions, who likes to direct prison theatricals and whose favorite novel is *The Princess Casamassima*. In making drama political they reduce politics to drama, and even the Provos are only too ready to substitute acting for action.

But, the book coolly suggests, Hood himself can't wholly avoid apprehending life as art. *His* favorite novel seems to be *The Secret Agent*, and though the stolen van der Weyden at first strikes him as a dull daub, it comes to fascinate him. He gradually learns how to see it even as he substitutes himself for the man he killed, by befriending, supporting, defending, and finally (in his way) loving Lorna Weech and her graceless child. And he finally recognizes that van der Weyden's portrait of the artist is a picture of himself in the role he's taken over from his victim: "He knew the face in the self-portrait now: it was the man he had killed, months ago, and he had become that man." If this is too fancy, still one admires Theroux for trying to find imaginative uses for his materials—the stolen picture in *The Blue Hammer* is only an item of deductive commerce, a fact Archer has to work with that's no more interesting in itself than any other of his clues.

Theroux's occasional over-ingenuities are hardly noticeable in the midst of a plot no less complex than any of Macdonald's. The threads of Hood's experience are as tightly interwoven as contemporary London itself, where everything leads to everything else. All over the city, walls and other public surfaces carry football slogans—CHELSEA FOREVER, SPURS WANK, ARSENAL RULE—but the last of these, Hood learns, is also a private joke of his bomb-maker friend Murf, who scrawls it wherever he goes to celebrate his army's aspirations to power. (This is more game than political action, and Murf can finally leave the IRA and become Hood's own man.) The stolen painting turns out to belong to Lady Arrow, but she, far from wanting to ransom it, is delighted that it can figure in a radical plot.

The accountant Ralph Gawber, whose ingrained respect for privacy saves him from violent death, finds his premonitions of national disaster—which he welcomes, now that his own neighborhood has gone Coloured—confirmed by frequent crossed telephone connections that thrust him into other people's business. Weech's frequenting of dog tracks points illogically but inescapably to the shabby house in the Isle of Dogs where Hood discovers the ignoble complicity of the Provo chieftain (Mayo's husband, as it emerges) with Weech's gang of gunrunners.

This is a nightmare world, where coincidence is never meaningless, where every act, however free in intention, recreates the anxieties it meant to escape from. Hood is both detective and criminal, faced with harder puzzles than the ones Gawber does in *The Times*:

> Once, when he had acted alone, it had all seemed very simple. His present anxiety was like a fear of crowds, the mob that would sweep him from his own motives. The origin of his doubt was the discovery weeks ago that he had made a passport for that wealthy actress he had taken a dislike to. So they were linked. But there was more: the painting stolen by the rich girl from the titled woman. They were all related! And what of Weech's arsenal? Was it also part of the family now? He resisted assigning it ownership as he had resisted

the complicated sympathy of kinship. Yet it was as if by degrees he was waking to the true size of his family and seeing it as so huge and branched it included the enemy. To harm any of them was to harm a part of himself. A family quarrel: if he cut them he bled.

Like Archer, Hood has to learn who's related to whom. But Archer doesn't bleed much when his enemies are cut—they're not, after all, *his* enemies but the Law's, and if he feels sorry for them he can't doubt that their punishment is just and necessary. Yet Hood the detective lets Hood the criminal get away. He does have to take on a "family" when he'd rather live alone and free like Archer, but he can at least limit his family, if only by rubbing out some of its less congenial members. His sense of a criminal world is aesthetic, not moralistic—it is bound together not by guilt but by connective patterns as mysterious and intriguing as those a painter's unknowable motives have put into his picture.

Hood in fact ends up like the hero of an older kind of American fiction, marked by his experience of a fallen society but heading off toward somewhere else where things may be a little better, with a good woman, a child, and a trusted companion in tow. Poor Archer can only go back to the office and wait for the next call. (In *The Blue Hammer* Macdonald for once permits him a love affair that looks like continuing after the book ends, but this seems an embarrassing betrayal of the rules.) His work is repeatable, and indeed a major appeal of the Archer stories, like Trollope or Scott or the Oz books, is that there are so many of them, and all so alike. But I can't imagine or wish for another novel about Valentine Hood, who here completes and exhausts his possibilities and will never again be interesting. *The Family Arsenal* is built out of books like Macdonald's, but Paul Theroux makes serious literary art out of a minor if durable genre without in the least condescending to his models or subordinating their kind of pleasure to his own.

# THE RED MENACE

*These next two pieces, read together, may look like a balancing act, though I wasn't aware of this when I wrote them. Both the books being discussed—Diana Trilling's cultural commentary and Robert Coover's polemical fantasy—seemed to me marred by political zeal: Trilling's zeal to defend the anticommunism of intellectuals in the 1950s and later, despite what I took to be its sorry historical consequences, and Coover's zeal to ridicule and punish that anticommunism more cruelly than I thought quite justified. Though my own views were probably closer to Coover's than Trilling's, both books seemed to misrepresent something, if for honorable reasons, and I tried to stress what did or didn't make sense in the texts.*

# Politics and Feeling
(1977)

THIS is the book Lillian Hellman's publishers refused to print unaltered, and so it comes trailing clouds of scandal. A new collection of essays by Diana Trilling ought to be read with dispassionate care, but I'm afraid that this is not the mood in which *We Must March My Darlings* will generally be received. Some will be ready to denounce or defend Trilling's views of our politics and culture even before they read them; others will be hoping for a peek into the private quarrels of eminent persons. One would regret this situation were it not so evident that she means many of these writings to be controversial, that the offenses they give are deliberate and principled assaults on what she sees as a profoundly disoriented cultural condition.

Trilling brings to the peculiar confusions of our time a moral and intellectual disposition that is strong and clear. Like what she says or not, one always knows who and where she is, what standards of judgment she applies to the case at hand. An acute observer of other people's limitations, she can, for example, put her finger squarely on the self-regarding softness of a countercultural performance like Timothy Leary's: "The essential quality he conveyed was that of a schoolmaster acting the master of ceremonies in a school show, a good-looking, tired, essentially vulgar, still-boyish teacher, histrionic, equally pleased with his popularity among his students and with the privileges of office which he could exercise as occasion demanded." Or, in the volume's most impressive and troubling essay, she can record her pained distaste for what now passes for education, and for life, at her own college, Radcliffe, while telling us, not without amusement, how she compulsively kept tidying up the living room of the dormitory she stayed at, whenever the messy students weren't looking.

There is more to admire, and like, in *We Must March My Darlings*. For all her disapproval of recent history's revolutionary moods, she is strongly sympathetic with the intentions, if not all the methods and rhetoric, of radical feminism, and similar generosity appears in her remarks about homosexuality and racial minorities. And her report on the young at Radcliffe leaves some room for their views, which, as in this discussion with a (male) student about the bad manners of his generation, sometimes upset her own ironic apple cart:

> D.T. Your middle-class generation was taught in nursery school that manners were internal, not the learning of forms.
> X. I was never taught that. We were told to behave like gentlemen.
> D.T. Were you really? What a nice retrograde upbringing you had!
> X. Never to *be* gentlemen. Not once was that mentioned. But to behave *like* gentlemen, as if it were some sort of imposture.

Their sexual freedom may be joyless, they may not know the dates of the French Revolution or what the Spanish Civil War was about ("I do know enough to know it was our fault!" one of them winningly snarls), but they have resources of their own, and Trilling isn't wholly unimpressed.

If such sharp and alert reporting were all it contained, the book could comfortably be taken as the important work of cultural interpretation it means to be. But it has not only an interpretive purpose but a polemical one, whether worked into a description of contemporary crisis, as in her account of the student revolt at Columbia in 1968, or given as outright assault on "revisionary" accounts of the fifties and sixties by such as Hellman, Jason Epstein, and Garry Wills. Here her writing sometimes grows shrill, her arguments unconvincing, and one's own politics may govern the response to her cases more than one wants them to. The chief text, and the source of the prepublication hurly-burly, is her rewriting of her answers (in 1967) to some symposium questions on "Liberal Anti-Communism Revisited" so as to take notice of Hellman's puzzlement in *Scoundrel Time* about how such "old, respected friends" as Diana and Lionel Trilling could have differed so strongly from her view of McCarthyism. Hellman's mild enough words—Trilling concedes that they were courteous and nonaccusatory—of course evoked the violent political passions of those sorry days, and Trilling's answer is fierce enough.

Hellman surely will not be glad to hear that she "has been able to countenance all the atrocities of Communist power since . . . the thirties" or that her famous letter to the House Un-American Activities Committee, offering to testify about herself but not others, was "a masterpiece of moral showmanship" which (because she pleaded the Fifth Amendment when the Committee refused her terms) won her "the permanent celebration of a moral fortitude which in actuality she did not implement." These being the sort of words with which men once provoked other men to take up the duelling pistol or the horsewhip, an outsider's first impulse may be simply to get out fast. But if the debate about whether "anti-anti-Communism" was the moral equivalent of Stalinism now seems dated, it conditions Trilling's (and others') sense of the present, and this is discussible.

A strong sense of history is a good thing, but when the past becomes a diagram of absolute right and wrong and the persons of history are conceived as unchangeably and totally identified by what they may once have thought or done, the historical sense is in trouble. Trilling is very severe with Hellman for supposing "that the error in her long unwavering acquiescence in Stalinism is disposed of in a phrase such as 'and there were plenty of sins in "Stalin Communism" and plenty that for a long time I mistakenly denied.'" But one may prefer a simple confession of error to what Trilling does with her own uneasiness, as a former official of the American Committee for Cultural Freedom, about that organization's monetary relations with the CIA, which, she indicates, were an open secret to insiders like her even then.

Trilling is quite unrepentant about her failure to protest at the time, because she could not then have known about the "dangerous usurpation of authority" the CIA was engaged in. Even though she knew that "in the strictest sense" it was a "breach of legality" for the CIA to fund secretly a domestic organization with no visible ties to intelligence or propaganda activities, this was excusable because we were waging ideological war against "the destruction of freedom in Europe and the East." A *good* CIA, as it then seemed to be, is justification enough.

But "breach of legality" is a nicer way of saying "crime," and Trilling is very hard on crimes farther from home. The violence of the police at Columbia in 1968 and at the Democratic National Convention later that year is glossed over because lawlessness was its provocation. The authorities in charge at either place can't be blamed, she says, for "the private rages of the men who enforce the law." But even if so general and collective a rage can properly be called "private," how can law enforcement accommodate *any* private feeling—rage or even love—without losing its sanction of legality? It is hard not to think that Trilling's view of the CIA and the cops is determined by ideology and not reason; the bad cause was winning sympathy from the excesses of the good one, and so (as with Joe McCarthy) those excesses needed to be played down for reasons of policy.

The trouble is that reasons of policy, insistently enough urged, can harden into reasons of principle, truths whose sanctity can condone any incidental violations of sense and language. Thus the HUAC–McCarthy witch-hunts were not all that bad, because some *real* Communists got accused along with those who weren't ones, and besides, our enemies do it too. Though McCarthyism was sadly "antiliberal," it was for Trilling preferable to Stalinism (the only known alternative?) because it merely deprived people of "very high-paid jobs" or gave them "a short jail term"; "no one was put to death for exercising his right of free speech." One is almost ashamed to ask why *any* punishment ought to be imposed for exercising a right.

Under ideological pressure of this sort, language has to surrender much of its ability to describe reality. Because Orwell (who well knew what ideology does to language) did suffer from his espousal of anti-Communist socialism after Spain, he can, under such pressure, be characterized as someone whose "reputation has never been allowed to recover," which is not true in the real world I know about, where his reputation could hardly be healthier. When Trilling says that "in the advanced literary community, and despite certain notable exceptions, liberal anti-Communism was not, and still is not the recommended path to professional success," the notable exceptions (Diana and Lionel Trilling among them) come at least as easily and numerously to mind as do successful persons with "radical" views.

"The most primitive expression of our current politics of sensibility," she remarks, "is the application of criteria of personal style to the making of political judgments." Certainly we have seen examples, from the Kennedys to now, of politics composed partly of personal style, and the complaint has its force. But with just a little nudging, words like "sensibility" and "style" can be made to mean rather too much. They can be made to include, for example, the pride in self and loyalty to others that made Lillian Hellman's response to persecution so humanly admirable, whatever Trilling thinks its political meaning may have been. They can include one's uneasiness about Trilling's reasons for opposing the Vietnam War: since our "overt military stance" was bad public relations in the rest of the non-Communist world, we would have done better to help the South Vietnamese with "money, technical assistance, arms" (help them do our fighting for us?). If the alternative to "sensibility" is only the old Cold War realism after all, one might wonder, if unfocused good feeling alone can't make good politics, whether rational prudence which so rigorously excludes humanity of feeling can do much better.

For Diana Trilling it clearly is an exclusion of such feeling, not an incapacity for it. When she's not wearing her full political armor, she writes about difficult subjects with a fine mixing of judgment and emotional responsiveness. It is at such moments, when she's not pursuing polemical missions, that she reminds us that the liberal anti-Communism of many American intellectuals had its honorable roots in the moral imagination, in a perception about Stalinism and its human effects that was not easily come by in the thirties and forties. At other moments, while I admire her persistence in her conception of the truth, I also wish that the world of her ideological categories could be less in command of the richer world she sees and feels.

# *The Nixoniad*
(1977)

When handling explosive objects, it is well to begin slowly and simply. So I'll say first that Robert Coover's *The Public Burning* is a long and fantastic fictional account of the events surrounding the executions for espionage of Julius and Ethel Rosenberg in 1953, that virtually all of the characters bear the names of historical personages, and that the principal narrator identifies himself as the then-Vice President of the United States of America, Richard Milhous Nixon. Already you may hear an ominous ticking sound.

As we know, the writing of even straight and sober history comes from fearing that we are potentially the victims of the past, that unless its meaning is better understood we may have to repeat its errors. The serious historical novel vivifies this intention by showing imaginary people more or less like us responding to real events in instructively adequate or inadequate ways. The historical fantasia, which writers like Ishmael Reed, E. L. Doctorow, and now Coover are giving us, show real people participating in, if not imaginary history, then at least history mythologized, broken up and recast into forms that may better indicate why it seems so sad, distasteful, or horrifying.

Horror and anger are the governing feelings in *The Public*

*Burning.* It isn't just that Coover sees the Rosenbergs as hapless victims of judicial injustice, people whose punishment cruelly exceeded any crime they did or didn't commit. Nor is it just that he pictures America in the McCarthy era as demonically possessed by anxiety and terror, aggressively in need of scapegoats through whom to exorcise its guilts and fears. Rather, he seems to see the Rosenberg case as evidence of a fundamental foulness in the American psyche that reveals itself plainly only when the national mask of pious rectitude slips a little.

Coover embodies this foulness in the person of "Uncle Sam," a sly, irascible, insufferably folksy fellow who sounds like a cross between Artemus Ward, Senator Claghorn, and Lyndon Johnson, endlessly embattled with "The Phantom," the elusive, protean menace of Communism or whatever else opposes our will. In one of his aspects Uncle Sam is a cartoon superhero who, with the help of movies, cowboy stories, and *Time* magazine (our Poet Laureate, whose utterances Coover prints as verse), fights within the national imagination for truth, justice, and the American way. He is also the unholy spirit of brute power that enters into our leaders, an incarnation which poor Nixon has to suffer quite literally, when Uncle Sam sodomizes him at the story's end.

Luckily for our patriotic self-esteem, Uncle Sam as Coover presents him is a crashing bore who carries on interminably in this vein:

> "I promised you a veritable day of havoc, my friend, and it ain't over yet! Nosiree, bob, I know what I's explanigatin' about, there'll be a disputacious hot time in the old town tonight, so you better get a grip on

# The Nixoniad

your braces, boy—when Jesus comes to claim us all, it's gonna be no place for skonks and cookie pushers! We're in for a terrible grumble and rumble and roar, a most strenuous and fearful concatenation of orful circumstances, so stay with the procession or you'll never catch up."

Lines like this do make it hard to remember that he signifies anything more than the American talent for garrulous bluster.

Uncle Sam presides over the less successful continuity in the book, a sequence of vignettes of America in midcentury built out of a careful analysis of the case against the Rosenbergs, a panoramic view of national and international conditions at the time, and a sour raking through of the cultural junk we now have such a nostalgic crush on. These episodes center upon the execution chamber at Sing Sing as magically replicated in Times Square, the crossroads of show biz, sexual license, the information media, tourism, and the general craziness of modern times. Here the nation assembles, from the public figures whose cynicism or ideological idiocy supposedly convicted the Rosenbergs, to the scared populace, who so badly want to be reunified through ritual bloodshed.

At its best, Coover's account of this saturnalia reads like a dazzling conflation of Blake's Prophetic Books, Pope's *Dunciad*, the Walpurgisnacht in *Faust*, and the grossest underground cartoons of today. I's especially fond of the man who comes out of a showing of *House of Wax* with his cardboard 3-D glasses still on and gets caught up in a revelry he can't see in focus but which sounds and feels strangely like the horror movie he just saw. ("God has not favored my undertakings," he muses, "my condition is not fundamentally sound.") But these episodes are too long-winded to be continuously enlightening about injustice and mass insanity. Even Coover's vast inventive powers can't keep us in touch with his anger indefinitely, and I rather guiltily found myself hurrying through these parts to get back to the narrative of Richard Nixon.

Astonishingly, Nixon is the most interesting and sympathetic character in the story. All the qualities that made the public figure so unlovable are present here—the smarmy self-righteousness, the suspicious insecurity within the strained affability, the appetite for success and power, the lack of physical and social grace, all of it. But while I cringe when he reflects that he's "a lot like Lincoln, I guess," I'm oddly touched when he supposes that "something [more] modern and Western" than the Washington, Lincoln, and Jefferson Memorials would be right for *his* monument but can only think of "the false fronts of the old cowtowns."

With the false fronts removed, Coover's Nixon is winningly capable of the uncalculated feeling (mostly malice, admittedly) that seemed so absent in the public figure, at least until we heard the tapes. He suggests that Eisenhower's celebrated pictures were drawn for him by others, so that Ike only had to paint by the numbers. At a moment of domestic disaffection, while Pat grimly cooks his breakfast, he wonders if her bathrobe might be inflammable like the ones Congress is legislating against. Fretting about that disastrously unshavable stubble, he wishes that politicians could still wear full beards, like Grant.

This Nixon, sharing the original's lack of motor skills, lurches through the book like some magnificently self-destroying silent-movie comic. He gets smeared with excrement, his zipper breaks, he is visited by erections at unpropitious moments, he gets his foot stuck under a taxi seat, he gorges to nausea on junk food, he plays doggie on his hands and knees for an unamused family circle, he innocently gives Uncle Sam an exploding cigar, he appears (after a stupefyingly tasteless account of a sexual encounter with Ethel Rosenberg) onstage in Times Square with his trousers down—a humiliation he converts to triumph by desperately improvising a "drop your pants for America" campaign, which ignites a wild public orgy in a blacked-out Manhattan. In a book which contains Jack Benny, Charlie McCarthy, the Marx Brothers, and some of the speeches of Dwight Eisenhower, Nixon is by far the funniest figure.

And, in a book that takes stern account of the official liberals of the time, Nixon is the only character who seriously doubts the Rosenbergs' guilt, suspects that the case against them is legally flimsy, and tries to do something to get them off. If the historical Nixon was under-endowed with such powers of sympathy, Coover does construct them out of something one can believe in, the idea that Nixon, lacking a strong center of selfhood, looked to other people for cues to what he thought or hoped he might be himself:

> Like my own father, Harry Rosenberg had tried to keep a store going . . . but had failed, fallen into abject poverty, and then, through hard work and tenacity, had fought his way back. . . . Like something out of a Horatio Alger story, except that Harry was a Socialist. . . . Little Julius had been very serious about his religion as a boy—we shared this. . . . He had led lessons and had even considered becoming a rabbi, just

as my mother had always thought I might become a
Quaker missionary. He was younger than me. . . .

Much of his attraction to the Rosenbergs is quite disreputable—his compassion for Ethel, who (he fancies) might have loved him for himself alone, has an alarmingly erotic basis, and he means to use them for his own political advancement. But there is understanding as well as contempt in Coover's portrait of his mind, and his hyper-alertness to signs that he may not be alone in his human plight gets just the right mixture of absurdity and pathos.

Coover brilliantly reconstructs a historical figure into a fictional one in order, I judge, to comment on too simply "personal" an idea of history. The evident villains of the past, villainous though they were, aren't the sources of evil but its agents, dupes, or victims. The evil is us, the aimless determination of a people to be up and doing something—anything—to assert our being and its power, rather than having to know too clearly what we are, and why. We need our Nixons, both because they can cater to our most reckless momentary desires and because they are so easy and gratifying to punish afterwards. In this sense, destroying Nixon and destroying the Rosenbergs gain *us* about equal credit, whatever the act cost them.

This, if I have it right, is a sufficiently demanding meaning to justify an extravagant, even wasteful expenditure of creative energy. As a work of literary art, *The Public Burning* suffers from excess: it is considerably too long and repetitive, it tests one's capacity for embarrassment too cruelly, its savage humor makes its sympathetic treatment of the Rosenbergs themselves, in all their hopeless ordinariness, sometimes seem mawkish by contrast. Nor, I hope, will many readers be thoroughly persuaded by Coover's contemptuous equation of our recent politics and folkways with the essence of the national character. But vigorous satire is always excessive and hurtful, and this novel is an extraordinary act of moral passion, a destructive device that will not easily be defused.

# ENEMIES

*In 1979 I seem to have written a lot on political violence: the next two pieces deal with commercial thrillers about "covert action" and conspiracy, and an uneven novel about terrorism by a distinguished writer. Life had by then grown terroristic enough for anyone, of course, and it was understandable that American writers and readers should be so interested in our newly-discovered vulnerability to the desires of disadvantaged foreigners and a few of our own weirder compatriots. "Terror in Freedonia" is about how some fairly bad novels tried to capitalize on the assumptions of terrified readers; "The Power of Art" deals with a more serious but still unconvincing treatment of similar materials. The underlying subject, I suppose, is the painful education of Americans in a school of humility none of us really wanted to enroll in.*

# Terror in Freedonia
(1979)

*I*T'S hard not to read reports of public crises and disasters the way we read novels of conspiracy and intrigue. Political upheavals, assassinations and mass atrocity, material shortages and monetary nightmares all invite the paranoid interpretation—somewhere there must be people who are doing this to us on purpose. History unquestionably *is* conspiratorially manipulated from time to time, but even if it weren't, we would want to think it was, hoping against hope that a secularized world can still, however dreadfully, make sense. If the CIA did not exist, it would probably be necessary to invent it, along with International Communism, Zionism, the Mafia, the PLO, the John Birch Society, OPEC, and bankers.

Although the CIA figures prominently in all the books I'm here concerned with, the governing mood of such fiction is of course much older than that beleaguered Agency. The mood goes back at least as far as the thrillers I read in childhood, stories by John Buchan, Edgar Wallace, Sax Rohmer, and E. Phillips Oppenheim in which Scotland Yard or some heroic agent saved Western civilization from nefarious cabals of gangsters, financiers, bolsheviks, or Chinamen. But these stories took place in never-never land; if a figure like Dr. Fu Manchu vaguely pandered to Occidental anxieties about the Boxers or Sun Yat-sen, opium, immigration, and the Yellow Peril generally, no one quite cared to admit it. In the last ten or fifteen years, however, such books have become more specific. Real public figures appear, often in scandalous postures, under their own or very similar names, historical events and fictitious ones mix and blur together, the bad guys and the good guys are hard to tell apart.

Writers like Robert Coover, E. L. Doctorow, Ishmael Reed, and—preeminently—Thomas Pynchon can accommodate this mood and its methods to serious fiction. But it's not good books but bad ones that best reveal the nature of a genre, and Edward Jay Epstein's *Cartel* is bad enough to be instructive. The time is 1953, Mohammed Mossadeq has nationalized the Iranian oil fields, and the international petroleum companies and the British and American governments are arranging his downfall at the hands of the CIA. *Cartel*, that is to say, is a romance founded very firmly in modern history.

Since modern history strikingly lacks heroes, however, Epstein has to invent one: Jacob Jasmine, tall, handsome, sexy, and brilliant young assistant professor of government at Harvard, an expert in the theory of coups d'état who's gullible enough to plan the overthrow and murder of Mossadeq while thinking he's just designing a new "game of nations" exercise. Since modern history doesn't offer many heroines either, Epstein supplies two smashing ones—a brainy young Oxford-trained logician who turns up in Jasmine's class, and her sister, at twenty-two "Britain's leading authority on pre-Raphaelite art." She has caught the fancy of the oil consortium's chief tactician and heavy, who keeps trying to press original Rossettis upon her. In due course Jasmine goes to bed with both sisters, when he's not tied up with the CIA's attempts to kill him.

Since Mossadeq did fall, Jasmine's struggle to save him hasn't much suspense. But Epstein diverts us by introducing real characters—Calouste and Nubar Gulbenkian, Enrico Mattei, John Foster and Allen Dulles, and H. Norman

Schwartzkopf all make appearances, some of them quite disreputable. Other characters may need a little translating. Might "Lord Crumonde" of "Anglo-Iranian Oil" suggest Lord Strathalmond of Anglo-Persian (as BP was then called)? Does "Kim Adams" of the CIA, scion of presidents, who serves up the Iranian coup, resemble Kermit Roosevelt? Could (just to show that I'm paying attention) the book's "Frank Bell" have something to do with Karl Twitchell of SOCAL? In any event, Epstein also drops the names of real people who don't figure in the story—Deterding of Shell, Teagle of Esso, the young Henry Kissinger, Anthony Eden, the Shah of Shahs, and so on—with a guileless gusto that reminds me fondly of Beerbohm's *'Savonarola' Brown*: "Enter BOCCACCIO, BENVENUTO CELLINI, and many others, making remarks highly characteristic of themselves but scarcely audible through the terrific thunderstorm which now bursts over Florence. . . ."

The styles of living of important people are treated as extravagantly as public history. In the tradition of Ian Fleming, Epstein's people are orgiasts of the higher consumption. There are the obligatory Rolls-Royces, the luxury hotels, the dinners at famous restaurants and grand private clubs like the Brook and the Metropolitan. Some of the menus are a little stomach-rumbling in their grandeur—how about gulls' eggs, game pie, and Stilton washed down with "a rich Petrus," or eggs Benedict and Courvoisier, or oysters, rack of lamb, and cherries jubilee? But the reader just back from Burger King will get the point.

Epstein's taste for splendor, however, sometimes breaks the thin bonds of credence that are needed to keep such a story connected with any kind of life. I won't even try to believe that, in 1953 or any other year, a *New York Times* reporter on the trail of a story his editors have never heard about could hope to charge his expense account for a two hundred dollar taxi ride from New York to Boston, dinners at the Sans Souci, and first-class flights to Teheran. Nor can I care about the fate of a supposedly sophisticated assistant professor who falls for the offer of an obscure British academic publisher (a CIA cover) to fly him to London, put him up at the Dorchester, and pay him a huge advance for his dissertation on political theory.

*Cartel* is in fact full of small blunders that keep spoiling its larger designs. Did people in Washington (!) and Cambridge (!!) take Joe McCarthy as lightly as the book's two brief and rather jocular references to him suggest? Did women wear body stockings in 1953? Did people say "nitty-gritty"? Were there paperback bookstores in Harvard Square? What is one to make of the description of that year's Harvard commencement, where women receive their B.A.'s in the Yard (not at Radcliffe), where all the doctoral candidates wear crimson robes (which were, I believe, adopted in 1955 and even then were uncommon, because you couldn't *rent* them), where the choir sings a "Bach oratorio" (the only work of Bach's that's called an oratorio by anyone is a set of six cantatas for Christmas, which sounds like an odd selection)? If Epstein had spent less time reading books on the oil industry and more time asking older people what 1953 was really like, *Cartel* would be easier to take. And why, by the way, does he establish a mysterious parentage for Jasmine, a bastard who knows of his father only that he's an "international tycoon" who likes flowers, and then never resolve the puzzle? Since the only likely candidates appear to be the all-too-historical Gulbenkians, maybe the publisher's lawyers have done some editing, but it looks as if nobody else has.

This is perhaps cruel to Epstein, an investigative journalist of some distinction who's trying his hand at fiction for the first time. But his book shows that it takes more skill and care than he's invested to conflate two popular literary modes. One is the bare-faced Flemingesque fantasia of global conspiracy, the technology of modern violence, and the virtues of toughness and expensive tastes, which spoofs both our anxieties about politics and war and our ability to live it up while we worry, and asks to be taken about as seriously as a Sigmund Romberg operetta. The other is the historical novel, which, whether serious or not, tries to show unremarkable people like us living through times of public crisis. The hybrid form means to suggest that we can learn about the world even as we participate in fantasies about being rich, powerful, and seductive. But these modes don't really blend, and even reasonably successful matings of them like Paul Erdman's *The Crash of '79* require some luck. Erdman happens to know a good deal about the shabbier aspects of international finance, and he has the advantage of wanting to get even with the Swiss government, multinational banks, currency speculators, and all the other parties to his own incarceration some years ago. Knowledge and passion help, and Epstein, who in the end allows the CIA to spare both Jasmine's and Mossadeq's lives for no clear reason except that the real Mossadeq, like Tiny Tim, did *not* die, seems lacking in both.

David Atlee Phillips's *The Carlos Contract* has knowledge and a little passion, if not much else. Phillips, an ex-CIA man and a public apologist for the Agency at a time when it badly needs one, tells a very timely story. A big international oil company is losing a lot of time and money because of the kidnapping and murder of its overseas executives, a nefarious effort that's being orchestrated by a single person, the "Carlos" we've read about in the papers. Since Carlos is also bumping off CIA station chiefs at an ungodly rate, the company and the Company get together and hire William ("Mack the Knife") McLendon, now in retirement but once "the best street man in the outfit," to find Carlos and make him disappear.

This too is a big-budget production. McLendon is no gourmet (he doesn't touch the "epicurean" dinner he's served on the Concorde), but he does know plenty about high-priced weapons and booze; at one endearing point he has to explain to an elegant friend from MI-6 that he's staying at the Holiday Inn because both Brown's and the Connaught were booked up. And above all, he gets around, flying this impressive circuit (all first-class, naturally) before his manhunt ends: Washington/New York/Washington/London/Bonn/London/Rome/London/Rio de Janeiro/Washington/Mexico City/Washington/London/Rio/Caracas/Miami/Washington/Hot Springs. In most of these places nothing is learned that a three-minute phone call wouldn't have uncovered, but lots of authentic local color is worked up. I wonder what the oil company's accountants made of McLendon's expense sheets.

The only interesting thing in the story is the climactic revelation that "Carlos" really isn't Carlos at all, but a rogue CIA man who has killed the terrorist and taken over his operations just to get some demented kicks. In effect, the contents of political action—the ideologies and demands for power that terrorism, for example, seems to express—drain away, leaving us to suppose rather comfortably that our public enemies are bad only for private reasons. I doubt that this reflects the CIA's or Phillips's own view of the world, but I can see why he may want us to imagine that there is no Carlos, no ideological terrorism, only irrational acts of personal aggression that can be dealt with by (to adopt what seems to be a term of the trade) putting the aggressive persons out of business. The world according to Phillips is a simple place, not terribly close to where we live. (One of the station chiefs Carlos rubs out is reassuringly named James Bond.) But I think that Phillips would like us to feel some connection with his world. McLendon doesn't want to kill the pseudo-Carlos when he catches him, he's basically nonpolitical, he even owns a Siqueiros lithograph. The Agency isn't really such a bad bunch when you get to know them. Indeed *The Carlos Contract* won't trouble readers who worry about the CIA, but only because it's so dull.

There is no CIA in Richard Condon's *Death of a Politician*, though there is something called the Secret Police (or SP), with headquarters in Semley, Maryland, which seems equally sinister. But Condon, who prefaces his story with Lord Acton's gloomy remark that "great men are almost always bad men," has more on his mind than mere spy-stuff. His domain is the dirty linen closets of politics and money (several of his novels deal with the rise and destruction of families very like the Kennedys), and his view—it might be called Condon's Law—is that when you don't know the whole truth, the worst you can imagine is bound to be close.

Here Condon considers the murder, in 1964 at the Waldorf Astoria, of Walter Bodmor Slurrie, former congressman and senator, vice president of the United States from 1952 to 1960, unsuccessful Republican candidate for the presidency in the latter year, a hypocrite well known for his dirty campaigns, his anticommunism, and his love of properly laundered money. If Slurrie sounds just a little like what's-his-name, there are some other familiar types around too—Richard Betaut, pint-sized former crime-busting DA and governor of New York, twice defeated for the presidency but still a power in the party, in whose apartment Slurrie's body is found; Nils Felsenburshe, current head of the richest family in the world, who may have political ambitions himself; David Arnold Dieter ("Dad") Kampferhaufe, revered military hero and president who never let Slurrie come upstairs in the White House or get off the helicopter at Camp David; Horace Riddle Hind, reclusive billionaire from out West with a taste for actresses, plain food, old movies, and soothing drugs, who buys up Las Vegas and bankrolls Slurrie's excursions into corruption; Eddie ("Kiddo") Cardozo, small-time Hispanic mobster from Miami who's Slurrie's guide, philosopher, and friend in many lucrative deals.

This is all bad enough, but Condon adds undreamed of horrors to what we knew or suspected about certain public figures. Slurrie got in with the Mafia by slipping them used tires when he worked in OPA, and they've directed his career ever since. Traumatized in his formative years by seeing his stern father copulating with a cow, Slurrie is helplessly impotent, and the ever-obliging Cardozo has had to beget his two sons. He won the vice-presidential nomination, despite Dad Kampferhaufe's loathing of him, because the Felsenburshes, Horace Hind, the Secret Police, and the Mob all wanted to have their man (he was *everyone's* man) at the center of things, where he could help organize or coordinate the Bay of Pigs, the Vietnam War, the assassination of the man who beat him in 1960, and the murder of Lee Harvey Oswald.

I'm not the first to observe that Condon's contempt for his readers almost matches his contempt for his characters. It's naughty of him to put the rise of Castro a decade too early, for example, just so that he can dump something else on the Kampferhaufe-Slurrie administration, and not all readers will find hilarious his insistence that Kiddo Cardozo sounds like Bill Dana playing "José Jimenez": "Lemme tell joo one thing. If I ever get my hans on the bahstair who kill Wullair I am firsz gun estoff him opp his own *culo*, then I am gun work on him with a axe. When you buss jawr ahss with a man for twenty years then some cogswawker come in an hit him you blow your rug. Oh, jess. . . ." (Notice that "joo" in the first sentence quickly changes to plain old "you.") And while some touches are reasonably diverting—I like the suggestion that Nils Felsenburshe never got nominated for president because he didn't need or want to be, that his failed candidacies were only to keep us from noticing that he'd been running the country all along—still there's not much political analysis. But then Condon isn't an analyst but an exploiter of our need to believe the worst. He does it with brio, but his books would be less fun than they are if one didn't suspect that he believes the worst too, that his pictures of a world of fools eternally at the mercy of knaves are also pictures of what, with anger and disgust, he takes to be the case.

Condon paints in broad strokes, and caricature has its uses, especially when it's truly ill-natured. But *Death of a Politician*, even more than *Cartel* or *The Carlos Contract*, persuades me that my anxieties about the public world are not usefully served by so flirtatious a blurring of art and life. Real toads belong in real gardens; when the idea of a world of enemies takes the form of fact, as it often enough does, it has to be dealt with seriously, but in so stylized and referentless a genre as the thriller, it seems better that the enemies too be imaginary.

# The Power of Art
(1979)

IN *Memories of a Catholic Girlhood*, perhaps her finest book, Mary McCarthy describes her youthful hopes for a career in an interesting way. Her ambition was literary, she says, but she does not put it as a yearning to become any one of the things she so notably *has* become, a novelist, a travel writer, a critical journalist of drama, literature, and public events; she wanted to be "a professional writer." Most people would call her a novelist, I suppose, but fewer than half of her 17 published books are works of fiction, and her latest, *Cannibals and Missionaries*, encourages the suspicion that she is best considered not as a novelist but as a professional writer who writes a novel from time to time—since the early 1950s, in fact, at steady intervals of eight years.

The earlier fiction had an obviously close relation to her own experience in the 1930s and early 1940s, as a bright young woman come down from Vassar to make her way in the literary-intellectual life of New York, with its fringes in Bohemia, Academia, and High Society. And her provincial, Catholic background gave her useful ironic leverage upon an intellectual life governed by Freud, Marx, and Literary Modernism. *The Company She Keeps, The Oasis, The Groves of Academe, A Charmed Life,* and (later) *The Group* are skeptical responses to "advanced" attitudes and modes of living that are nonetheless recognized as attractive and necessary alternatives to what otherwise might have been. Had she not been orphaned in childhood, she equally suggests in *Memories of a Catholic Girlhood*, her life would probably have taken a very different turn: "I can see myself married to an Irish lawyer and playing golf and bridge, making occasional retreats and subscribing to a Catholic Book Club. I suspect I would be rather stout." The earlier fiction, with its cool, malicious portrayal of recognizable individuals and types, suggests a writer determined not to be fooled and utterly possessed by a life that nevertheless represents a welcome escape from narrow, spiritless possibilities.

This fascinating sense of self-division is much less evident in *Birds of America* and, now, *Cannibals and Missionaries*. Her interest has been shifting from personal history to public history, as her writings on Vietnam and Watergate suggest too. But such a change doesn't ensure stronger novelistic performance, and while *Cannibals and Missionaries* is a considerable book, full of intelligent speculation about serious contemporary issues, it is not a terribly successful work of fiction.

The story is both simple and timely. An airliner flying from Paris to Teheran is hijacked by political terrorists, who eventually hole up with their hostages in a prepared stronghold in a remote part of Holland. The hostages consist of two rather antipathetic groups of (mostly) Americans—a gaggle of liberal human-rights advocates on their way to see what the Shah is doing to his political enemies (the time is around 1975), and a clutch of wealthy art collectors going to tour Iranian archaeological sites. The terrorists, an oddly mixed bunch of Dutch, German, Palestinian and Latin American types, evidently had planned to bag the liberals, perhaps on a tip from the SAVAK: the millionaires are an unexpected bonus.

This is of course the stuff of thrillers, and McCarthy does provide some suspense and a climax of slam-bang violence.

And she has worked hard to achieve the accuracy of surface behind which the larger improbabilities of this genre may decently conceal themselves; in a preface she thanks a number of people, from Hannah Arendt to James Angleton, for helping her learn about such things as land reclamation in Holland, Dutch politics, airplanes, Iran, the art market, and hijacking. But as a story of real-life terror, *Cannibals and Missionaries* is plagued by dubious details. In such a story it matters that, for example, an Air France 707 is represented as having 2x2 seating in tourist, or that a very prominent U.S. Senator is shown as embarking on a politically sensitive humanitarian mission without aides, security people, or press coverage. Less specifically, perhaps, one wonders about a president of a New England women's college whose hatred of rich people is not just violent but vocal—how in the world does her school raise money?

More seriously, McCarthy doesn't make her terrorists and their motives seem very convincing. Their formal conditions for the release of the liberal hostages are that Holland withdraw from NATO and end diplomatic relations with Israel. No government could accept such demands, and no serious terrorists could expect to gain them, yet these really mean it, and they have no secondary positions—money, safe-conduct to Libya or whatever—to bargain toward. McCarthy suggests that they're showing off, turning terrorism into a work of art for the admiration of friendly competitors like "Carlos" or the PFLP, but such a notion removes the novel pretty far from real cases.

The difficulty increases as McCarthy turns "terrorism as art" into a plot that literally involves works of art. The hijackers, led by a former art student, get the bright idea of offering to ransom the rich collectors for their collections, to be flown in from New York and landed by helicopter. The theory is that, while the Dutch government might eventually decide to risk the captives' lives by assaulting the farmhouse they're held in, no government could risk the destruction of irreplaceable paintings: "The masterpieces would not only guarantee the security of the command post; they would be replacing their owners as hostages. Threats to execute one or all of them would have more powerful leverage than threats to execute one or all of the present company; the very notion of such an infamy would cause a thrill of horror to run round the civilized world."

Here an intriguing idea is literalized into nonsense. It is quite true that bourgeois culture places an immensely high value, monetary and otherwise, on unique works of art, and "civilized" people probably will feel something about (say) the destruction of a Rembrandt they've never seen that they may not feel about the destruction of persons they've never met. (McCarthy cites the case of the Kenwood House Vermeer, stolen by the IRA with a threat to mutilate it gradually; but the demands were not met, and the picture eventually turned up more or less intact.) It is surely *not* true, however, that peril to masterpieces would deter attack by any even nominally democratic government in a way that peril to human hostages, particularly rich and influential ones, would not. Such governments must answer to voters, and voters who care more about great works or art than about human lives are (fortunately, I should think) a small minority in any country. Once the hostages were replaced by paintings, those with the gravest worries would not be the governors but the insurance companies.

Even if McCarthy were right about the power of art, her story would be in trouble. The deal is that the paintings will only ransom their owners, not the liberal "missionaries." But since the latter group includes an American senator who once ran for President and the Leader of the Opposition in the Dutch parliament, it can safely be assumed that the governments in question would never permit the delivery of the art works, which by McCarthy's reasoning represent their only bargaining points, until the release of *all* the hostages is assured. I shudder to imagine the political consequences, in the real world, of a decision that allowed a few rich people to buy their safety while leaving a group of statesmen, clergymen, educators, and writers in mortal peril.

Nor does McCarthy's picture of how hostages and terrorists get along together seem very credible. Her theory is, to be sure, based on reported fact—we're told, and it sounds sensible, that in such situations a kind of rapport can develop between captives and captors, a mutual sense of shared discomfort and danger that can somewhat reduce their natural animosity. But I doubt that a couple of days of propinquity would turn the tone of things into that of summer campers and counselors:

> "We shall return now," she announced abruptly, seizing Denise's arm and wheeling about. Cries of protest arose. "Oh, Greet, that's not fair," remonstrated Aileen. "Jeroen *said* we were to have thirty minutes. We all heard him. And we've only been out ten." "Another five," pleaded the pastor. "It's such a wonderful day. You need the fresh air, Greet. It'll put roses in your cheeks."

And there's something both unreal and strangely condescending about McCarthy's way of depicting the non-European hijackers—Palestinian and Latin American—as, in effect, amiable, childlike, protective *servants* of both their comrades and the captives, as if it all were something like a rather edgy house-party down on the old plantation.

Depending on one's own political and moral outlook, it is possible to think of terrorists as common criminals, as crazed fanatics, or as tragic victims or heroic agents of significant political purposes. In each view they figure as extremely dangerous persons. But McCarthy's terrorists are cream-puffs. Until the novel's finale, whose lethal consequences are quite accidental, the only living creature they kill or even wound is a cat; when they need a dead body to show the world they mean business, they shoot up a hostage who's already dead of a heart attack; when another victim is needed, they agree to pass over the available people and the valuable Cézannes and Vermeers, and destroy a mere Marie Laurencin. To the extent that it seeks to represent a frightening reality, *Cannibals and Missionaries* is fairly preposterous.

The book does better in describing personalities, or personality-types, under the pressures of bewilderment, anxiety, and fear. Here some significant categorizing is detectable. McCarthy has little use for American WASPS, of whatever political or social persuasion: the liberal college president is abysmally self-centered; the humanitarian Episcopal priest is an utter fool; the rich collectors are mostly fascistic snobs. (But it helps if you're old, like the dimly decent-minded Episcopal bishop, or both old and epicene, like the closet-Democrat connoisseur Charles Tennant, one of the book's nicest characters.) Jews and foreign-born Calvinists do better: McCarthy clearly approves of Sophie Weil, the attractive journalist; she feels some sympathy for Victor Lenz, the quite unattractive Middle-East specialist with CIA connections; she can tolerate a Scottish Presbyterian like Archibald Cameron, now a (yes) dour Oxford historian, and she's fascinated by Jeroen, the leader of the hijackers, whose rigid Dutch-Protestant upbringing drove him to art studies, radical politics, terrorism, and finally a recognition of what the sin of despair is all about.

But the two characters McCarthy likes best are both failed (or failing) Catholics, as well as being lawyers, successful politicians, poets, and men of the world. One, Senator James Carey, comes uncomfortably close to being a portrait of the author's namesake, Eugene, and it's enough to say here that for all Carey's charm, sophistication, and wisdom, his vanity and cynicism permit him to be killed off at the end. His counterpart, the Dutch statesman Henk Van Vliet de Jonge, has all of Carey's virtues and none of his flaws; he's also a better poet, and he gets out of the story with only a serious concussion. Carey and Van Vliet are the right spectators for the drama McCarthy means to present. Unlike the other hostages they know how the world works, they can keep cool under pressure, they are humanly interested in their nominal enemies, they know as artists that larger issues are at stake in immediate actions. (If Mary McCarthy *had* married that "Irish lawyer," one suspects that he would have been both bookish and politically ambitious.) Though Van Vliet's faith is lost and Carey's is in some doubt, both have been prepared to see the secular world in the concerned yet detached way the author sees it too.

This may be rather too convenient for McCarthy's purposes, and rather too hard on all the people in the book who haven't had the advantage of a Catholic upbringing. And I wonder if the statesman-poet, our Sidney and our perfect man, is quite as credible a type as he used to be; in a world like ours, unfortunately, it seems likely that one of the talents will eventually consume the other. But though I'm not convinced that the cultivated politician is the finest type our age affords, I must admit that Carey and Van Vliet (and the terrorist Jeroen, their peer on The Other Side) largely escape the outlines of caricature enclosing most of the novel's characters and achieve a considerable semblance of complex life.

I can't imagine not being interested in anything written by Mary McCarthy, and *Cannibals and Missionaries* has pleasure and instruction to give to anyone who values wit, intelligence, and seriousness of purpose. But as a realistic novel it's full of holes, and I wish that she had given us her thoughts on art, violence, and the inadequacy of most secular roles in some more direct, or more oblique and fantastic, form.

*"Stage and Screen" is another study in the colliding of theory and experience. Robert Brustein's history of his Deanship of the Yale Drama School gives a fascinating account of a principled idea of American theater under fierce pressure from public history, a pressure that created "drama" off-stage as well as on. Though Brustein's was in many ways an honorable performance, it will be clear that I felt more comfortable with a (television) critic like Michael J. Arlen, who was less sure of what the age (and the medium) demanded, and more able to respond to the complexity of immediate cases.*

# Stage and Screen
(1981)

LIFE is always hard to distinguish from the prevailing ways of representing or reproducing it. Robert Brustein's subject is theater and Michael J. Arlen's is television, but both writers in effect ask how intellectual seriousness can find living space within a cultural medium that seems hostile or (worse) indifferent to its traditional premises.

As its title implies, *Making Scenes* is the story of Brustein's sometimes melodramatic tenure as dean of the Yale School of Drama and director of the Yale Repertory Theatre from 1966 to 1979, a period which, for all its successes and satisfactions, he and others found painful. Some of the pain was history's fault; those were hard years for universities, the arts, the nation. But as he not very contritely acknowledges, Brustein brought to history certain professional intentions and personal qualities that made things harder than they might have been if some gentler or more diplomatic soul had been running the show.

Certainly his idea of how a university should be involved in theater wasn't calculated to win him many friends in New Haven. Hired by Kingman Brewster to revitalize the torpid Drama School as best he could, he had no intention of serving the usual constituencies. Undergraduates were from the start offended by being denied any contact with what was, after all, a graduate program, and Brustein's refusal to accommodate their interests irked many administrators and faculty members too. Nor were the Drama School's own acting students delighted to find that *they* were for the most part excluded from performing with the pros of the Repertory Theatre, for Brustein the most important of the various theaters at the school. (Stella Adler, brought in to teach acting, in fact took the position that her students shouldn't act at all, not even in student productions.) The school's alumni were mostly dismayed by Brustein's changes of professional emphasis, his insistence that he was not there to train teachers for college drama departments or performers and technicians for commercial theater, film, or TV. Nor, he reports himself saying, did he have any interest in entertaining the residents of New Haven, though he sounds a little bitter about the preference of many of the Yale faculty for the somewhat less austere Long Wharf Theatre.

What he did have in mind was a conservatory, on the model of Juilliard or the Old Vic School, to train actors and directors for professional "resident theaters" around the country. This admirable design is worth examining, since it brought him a good deal of grief before he was through at Yale.

Brustein, like other theater people, was attracted to the idea of professional resident theater on a national scale because it pointed to a way of escape from the unattractive alternatives that dominated live drama in America. On the one hand was an almost wholly commercial professional theater, doing trivial popular plays or tame classics, more or less competently, on Broadway, in road companies, or in summer stock; on the other was the hopeful amateurism of the stage-struck, in college or community playhouses. Resident theater on the European model promised a happy marriage of trained capability and artistic adventurousness of a sort that commercial theater couldn't afford to propose even if it wanted to. More generally, it offered a way of imagining a serious dramatic culture which could oppose the slick mediocrity of American show business. As a conservatory, Yale would be a stronghold for the dramatic wing of the "adversary culture" which traditional intellectuality represented.

Brustein certainly had the intellectual's distaste for popular culture. Early in his deanship, he admits, he diverted to other uses a grant for a television script-writing program from ABC, because he "was uninterested in TV." He struggled to keep New York reviewers at arm's length, in part (he winningly allows) because he mistrusted his own taste for notoriety, but more because he disliked having Yale productions written about as if they were in competition with Broadway. Although he seems glad that successful young actors were trained at Yale, Ken Howard, Talia Shire, Meryl Streep, and Henry Winkler among them, his rather reserved comments on their later careers in television and film suggest that he may feel at least mildly betrayed. That was not what he meant at all.

And of course the popular was for him more than just a professional menace during his early years at Yale. His style as the unacademic, ungenteel, New York-based literary intellectual, his commitment to advanced modes of theater, and his vocal opposition to the war in Vietnam made it at first easy for some in New Haven to think him a dangerous radical; but on his own territory he was anything but that. He believed that participatory democracy cannot well serve instruction in a difficult art and that a good conservatory must be an authoritarian place, where masters demonstrate and teach, and apprentices obey and learn. At the center of *Making Scenes* is Brustein's account of how he resisted the efforts of many students (and faculty) to convert the Drama School, and Yale itself, into a functional expression of the "New Politics," which for him meant something like his professional bête noir, Julian Beck's Living Theatre. He has written before, in *Revolution As Theatre* (1971), of Yale's May Day strike during the Black Panther trials in 1970, and the new account is more reflective and sober than that rather shrill book. He seems more willing to understand the views of his antagonists, a little readier to see that his own performances may have been more provocative than was necessary.

Brustein's is an evidently combative temperament, but his career at Yale expresses more than a thorny personality. His wife once teasingly called him "the Great Right Father," and his attitudes toward the theater and the world, and, even more, his habit of codifying those attitudes and then defending them fiercely against all comers, suggest a tendency to allow life to be dominated by theory, and a continual need to be *right*. At one characteristic moment, black students in the Drama School protested his plan to produce Sam Shepard's *Operation Sidewinder*, which they considered, however unfairly, to be racist, and some of Brustein's colleagues urged him to cancel the production.

> When I tried to point out inconsistencies in their position, they told me that personal opinions were less important than placating the black students. Two older white radical students, with whom I had warm relations, also urged me to withdraw the play, in view of the fact that this was a time of crisis. "A lot of students feel blacks have been oppressed for two hundred years, and should be given what they ask for as a form of reparation. The play doesn't matter. It's more important to give the black students a sense of self."
> 
> "Does that mean we should burn the books?" I asked them.
> 
> "No," one answered. "Just put them on the shelf until a better time."

However often one has heard such discussions, the situation in question usually turns out to be more complex than its rhetoric allows. Brustein takes the part of liberal theorist, concerned with "positions" and "pointing out inconsistencies" and entirely ready, in a familiar device of argumentative overkill, to enlarge canceling a show into something approaching a Hitlerian literary conflagration. His "radical" opponents are given the part not of true radicals but of moralistic mushheads, bursting with the cant of bourgeois guilt and positively eager to trim their principles to the fashion of the time. It would be hard to question the rightness of Brustein's attitude—the "radical students" in fact don't deny it—yet his insistence that it be established as "a position" diminishes its power, particularly since, caught in an irony whose depth he may not have fully sensed, he next tells us that the play was canceled after all, at the author's request:

> Under the terms of our contract with Shepard, we had a legal right to produce the play, even without his consent, but I wouldn't do this. . . . One of the principles I was trying to defend was the artist's freedom from external constraints. Staging *Operation Sidewinder* against the playwright's wishes was just as much a violation of this principle as trying to suppress it. I realized that I was defeated—and on an issue of supreme importance to me. I had lost the fight for freedom of the stage at Yale.

The trouble with basing too much, too rigidly, on principles, obviously is that good ones sometimes collide when they are put into practical motion. Brustein had indeed lost a fight, but one doubts that "freedom of the stage at Yale" was at stake, since the Rep continued to function, without further reports of censorship, for another decade.

Brustein's crustiness was based on a noble dream of a theater liberated from popular taste and commercial venality, free to discover and criticize the unexamined terms of the national life. If history was the immediate problem, it may not, however, have been the only thing that opposed his principles and theories. For him there was a necessary gap between stage and spectators, a barrier against any direct connection between what is represented in art and what is felt and done outside the theater. He believed, he says, in intellectual and artistic "revolt" but not in social and political "revolution," since he always felt sure that "trying to change society was impossible without a change in the basic nature of humankind." Hence, I suppose, the apparent paradox within his critical career. In *The Third Theatre* (1969) he could praise plays like *Viet Rock, America Hurrah, Dynamite Tonite,* and *MacBird* because they subverted prevailing theatrical formulas and methods, not because they pointed to possible new actions offstage. And when the university itself turned into a kind of revolutionary drama, he found himself vehemently opposed to much that happened, becoming, as *Revolution As Theatre* records, something like the town scold, unlikely to persuade no matter how sound his argument.

*Making Scenes* is, to be sure, more than the continuing saga of one man's political and cultural intransigence. It gives a detailed record of a valuable and influential theatrical experiment, a moving account of personal affection and loss in the untimely death of his wife, and some fascinating glimpses of institutional politics, most notably in Brustein's descriptions of his public dispute with President Giamatti upon his leaving Yale, over whether he was being fired or simply not reappointed. But at its center, and most interesting of all, is a portrait of an unaccommodated and embittered intellectual man, relentlessly hostile to the conceptions of the majority culture and yet deeply troubled when opposing conceptions, his own included, escape from the laboratory of art and theory to run free through the marketplace.

For me, Brustein's distinctions between what is serious and what is popular are too rigid, just as his approach to theatrical production, as he describes it, sounds too clerkly, as in his deciding that *The Wild Duck* has photography as its "central metaphor" and his staging of the play "as if it were a gigantic black-and-white photograph," with a huge lens replacing the curtain, flashes going off, and characters freezing in stills. But there's also something rather splendid about Brustein's single-minded devotion to his understanding of seriousness; if his kind of intellectuality seems doomed to lose many of its battles against the realities that now confront it, in *Making Scenes* he loses surprisingly gracefully, with touches of ruefulness and self-mockery that seem, in such a personality, particularly attractive.

Michael J. Arlen's television criticism in *The New Yorker* also represents a literate and serious mind responding to a culture that often disappoints even its most modest hopes. Unlike most TV reviewers, Arlen keeps his distance from both the networks and the pretensions of much public television; but he differs from Brustein in not having divided up culture into wholly distinct provinces before cultural events take place, and in not being so sure that anything popular must be somehow unworthy.

*The Camera Age* begins, in fact, with a cautious plea for a medium that high-minded people frequently condemn as being dangerous to our social, cultural, and personal health. This "huge, shared, strangely experienceless experience" is, he argues, not simply a hypnotic, manipulative, misleading influence on the lives of all who participate in it. When we consider not ideal possibilities but actual cases, television appears, for example, to be beneficial for lonely people, especially old ones, compensating them for a loss of human contact which TV after all hasn't caused. And though it exposes children to vulgarity and hard-sell hype, it also gives them "choice as well as freedom of access, and also provides them—within the glowing, flickering perimeter of the TV set—something that throughout history the young have badly needed: a place of their own to exist in, temporarily untalked to, undefined, unimproved." Not all questions are answered by such a remark. *How* will they exist in there? What habits of thought and language will they absorb? When they're old enough not to need this refuge, will they be able to get out? But this is an appealingly thoughtful and unexcited kind of voice, more intent on human cases than on scoring theoretical points.

Arlen does propose a small-scale theory about how we live with television. It is, he plausibly suggests, a "porous" or "permeable" medium, quite unlike print, visual art, or performed music or drama or even film. It does not demand our full attention but affably allows us to chat with the family, wash the dishes, talk on the phone, read, or do homework while remaining in some kind of touch with what's on the screen. He doesn't say so, but I presume that this porosity owes something to TV's being free or, for cable users, at least much cheaper than live shows or concerts, continuous (if you miss part of one program, another will soon follow), duo-sensory (you can watch without listening, or vice versa), and so easy to get to, and leave. The set appears here as a kind of close relative you don't have to be too polite to, Big Brother stripped of his charismatic authority, as it were. The relationship will improve, Arlen hopes, as we continue to learn ways of "talking back" to television, not only through phone-in talk shows but through new technologies like satellite transmission for public broadcasting and pay-cable networks, which should greatly enlarge our cultural choices, and literal talk-back devices like the Qube system, with its array of "response signal" buttons to push. But even now, while the flow remains essentially one-directional, he sees TV as something less than inherently menacing.

Porous or not, however, television does convey something, and when considering particular programs or genres, Arlen's good cheer often subsides. The range of *The Camera Age* is not wide: of the twenty-five pieces to which I'm able (sometimes rather arbitrarily) to assign a main subject, thirteen deal with news or other "fact" broadcasting, including one "docudrama," and eight with dramatic series or films, from *Charlie's Angels* and *Baretta* to PBS versions of literary classics. This leaves a scant one article each for sports, showbiz (the Oscar awards), game shows, and talk shows, and except for passing remarks, nothing at all on a huge if mostly uninspiring portion of what most people, including *New Yorker* readers, watch—day-time drama, comedy-variety shows, cartoons and other children's programs, situation comedies, westerns, religious programs, old movies, pop music and dance for the teen crowd, ethnic programming. It's understandable that a serious critic should give most of his attention to the "higher" ranges of TV, where it ought to be doing good things for us, but the evident fact that it mostly is *not* doing much good in those ranges gives Arlen ample opportunity to chide and deplore, as he seldom does with the humbler stuff.

He's easy on *Dallas* for example, describing it as an interesting reflection of the formlessness of contemporary manners. Unlike most soap operas, it give the audience no sense of what rules pertain, so that characters seem not so much to be misbehaving as to be changing their social identities at will, as if there were no significant conventional resistances to impulse or desire. This is, I suppose, a subtle way of saying that *Dallas* is morally repellent, but Arlen's inclination, or tactic, is to save such straight, square talk for more pretentious occasions, like the public television adaptation of *The Scarlet Letter*, which rouses the print-culture moralist in him to outrage:

> One has the impression that the mass media, which are largely visual, are in the process of trying to perpetuate [in a calmer mood, would he have written "perpetrate"?] an illusion: the illusion being that

culture is somehow neutral as to form and can therefore best be communicated and recommunicated by means of the most popular forms of the day. Thus, some of the great literary spirits of our civilization have been made unwitting participants in a curious sort of visual vs. literary Capture the Flag contest, in which the visual team lately appears to have the upper hand, drawing bigger crowds and winning fatter purses. Will the visual team continue to forge ahead, chewing up Homer and Dante and the Oxford English Dictionary and spitting them out in ten-part installments, each verified for historical accuracy by a battery of academics and scripted so as to be easily comprehensible to a ninth-grade audience? One will have to wait for the twenty-first century to find out.

These weighty fulminations transform a fair point, that this particular adaptation was both inept in itself and a warning about how not to make TV out of novels, into one that I think Arlen himself would at another time agree is stuffy and false, that good literature is too sacred for visual art to meddle with at all.

On the whole I'm glad that he saves most of his big guns for nominally serious television that goes wrong. As a fairly passive fan of *60 Minutes*, for example, I am properly corrected when Arlen (who also likes it, but more skeptically) takes the trouble to look into a story which seemed to reveal grave moral and political corruption in Wyoming and finds shocking manipulation of fact and rhetorical distortion. His warnings about confusing investigative journalism with the prosecutorial power, which the founding fathers wisely did not confer upon the press, are strongly argued, and it's good to know that someone is trying to watch the reporters so carefully. We can, after all, deal with *Dallas* by ourselves.

Arlen's successes are impressive for their simplicity,

meaning that they seem to remind us of something we think we knew before we read him but probably didn't. He observes that the Reagan-Carter debate was both disappointing and strangely affecting because for once we got to see both men without the benefit of the technology that had enclosed and dehumanized them in campaign spots and news clips. Without montage, voice-over, or music, they seemed sad, lonely, anxious, like students taking their SATs. When he wonders why talk shows have "hosts," perfunctorily going through the rituals that appease our fear of strangers, vaguely apprehended presences come into focus—Merv Griffin is revealed, for example, as "the doctor or lawyer who has been more or less trapped into giving a party but is still trying to have a good time," and Dinah Shore as "the wife, or widow, of some grander, absent chairman of the board." And Arlen, who is enviably perceptive about the young, goes on to remark that their formless way of entertaining—the fluid guest list, the vagueness about when and even where, the uncertainty about who's in fact giving the party—may indicate a positive effect of television, which demystifies strangers and makes ritualized sociability unnecessary in the brave new world it has educated.

For the sake of such fine things one can easily forgive Arlen his occasional lapses—his way of reaching for the fancy analogy or the broad satiric tone, or offering a far-fetched explanation when a simple one is close at hand. The wild approval he heard in a movie theater when Peter Finch put down news broadcasting in *Network* must surely have had less to do with the audience's subliminal awareness that watching TV is masturbatory, as he thinks, than with their feeling, in 1976, that they were fed up with fifteen years of hearing bad news. Despite such moments, which of course fail not from obtuseness but from an excess of wit, Arlen's writing encourages the hope that the criticism of popular culture is fit work for strong minds, and that it can be conducted without too much worry about what's supposed to be serious and what isn't.

*John Updike's idea of America seems to me clearest and richest in the series of novels that began with* Rabbit, Run, *continued in* Rabbit Redux, *and* Rabbit Is Rich, *and (as I half jokingly predicted) became a quartet in 1990 with* Rabbit at Rest. *Just about everything is there somewhere—politics, sex, religion, family romance, economics, the surface details of ordinary experience—and it helps a wondrously fluent writer to have to displace his own sense of life into the consciousness of an anti-self like Harry Angstrom, so much less articulate and gifted than the author, though humanly no less significant. The suspicion lingers in some quarters that Updike isn't quite what we want a major novelist to be—why isn't he black, or Jewish, or a woman, or crazy? how can he write so much, so well, so readably? shouldn't he be suffering more?—and I enjoyed an occasion to praise him without much embarrassment.*

# *Updike's Rabbit*
(1981)

JOHN Updike became an "important" writer, as we say, with his second novel, *Rabbit, Run*, published in 1960 and still, twenty-one books later, one of his best performances. Since then, Updike's imagination has lingered upon Harry Angstrom, called "Rabbit" in his days of glory as a high school basketball star; *Rabbit Redux* (1971) found him a decade older, beset by the troubles and confusions that beset us all in the late 1960s, and now a third book, *Rabbit Is Rich*, whose opening words are "Running out of gas," shows him middle-aged and slowing down some, in what, once again, we recognize to be the present. One hadn't quite understood that a series was in progress, and Updike's pleasant surprise suggests that the new work needs to be considered as part of a larger whole.

*Rabbit, Run* now seems distinctly a novel of the 1950s, if only because it takes so little account of the public terms of life in its time. The setting, a small Pennsylvania city in 1959, is lovingly observed, and the culture of common experience—popular songs, television shows, and the like—is duly acknowledged, but it is Harry Angstrom's sense of self, his inward spiritual being, that draws the novelist's attention and energizes his remarkably lyric style. At twenty-six, with high school, local athletic stardom, and stateside military service during the Korean War behind him, Harry, a printer's son, has impregnated and then married a girl somewhat above him in the social scheme. Harry and Janice have a small son and another child on the way; they live in a drab walk-up while Harry tries to sell kitchen gadgets and Janice neglects the housework, drinks too much, and nurses her discontent. Harry is on the run throughout the novel, from Janice to Ruth, a good-hearted, overweight prostitute, from Ruth back to Janice when their daughter is born, and eventually from both of them, when Janice accidentally lets the baby drown in the bath tub and Ruth reveals that she's now pregnant too.

This familiar tale, of possessive women and escape-artist men, has little to do in particular with the 1950s in Middle America. It has much more to do with the then rather fashionable interest announced by the novel's epigraph from Pascal: "The motions of Grace, the hardness of the heart; external circumstances." Updike intends to look through Harry's apparent human inadequacies, his way of disappointing or hurting those who would love him or at least welcome his love, toward the idea that fascinates the book's rather feckless clergyman, Jack Eccles, that (as Harry himself cheerfully reports it) "'I'm a mystic. . . . I give people faith.'" In all the novels it is suggested—Updike is too canny to insist on it—that Harry, resolutely commonplace in most other ways, has a special spiritual gift, however poorly he understands or articulates it, a persistent sense of what William James in *A Pluralistic Universe* wittily called "a more": "The believer finds that the tenderest parts of his personal life are continuous with a *more* of the same quality which is operative in the universe outside of him and which he can keep in working touch with, and in a fashion get on board of and save himself, when all his lower being has gone to pieces in the wreck."

James's terms are helpful in making out Harry Angstrom. Though his "lower being," the part of him that *ought* to be more observant of what his wife, his lovers, his parents, his children expect and need from him, does continually go to pieces, he at least dimly sees that "the tenderest parts of his personal life" participate in something more outside of him and that he can at least hope to save *himself*. At moments of ordinary pleasure—playing basketball or golf, gardening, feeling intimacy with his children,, and above all performing the acts of physical love—Harry's life is obscurely but deeply touched by intimations of continuity with some savingly larger presence or purpose, intimations that human time does not erase, as Updike suggests (for example) by making Harry's response to his new-born granddaughter at the end of *Rabbit Is Rich* plagiarize from what he felt when he first saw his ill-fated baby daughter twenty years before:

> The tiny stitchless seam of the closed eyelid runs diagonally a great length, as if the eye, when it is opened, will be huge and see everything and know everything. . . . In the suggestion of pressure behind the tranquil lid and in the tilt of the protruding upper lip he reads a delightful hint of disdain. She knows she's good. What he never expected, he can feel she's feminine, feels something both delicate and enduring in the arc of the long pink cranium.
>
> (*Rabbit, Run*)

> The baby shows her profile blindly in the shuddering flashes of color from the Sony, the tiny stitchless seam of the closed eyelid aslant, lips bubbled forward beneath the whorled nose as if in delicate disdain, you can feel in the curve of the cranium she's feminine, that shows from the first day.
>
> (*Rabbit Is Rich*)

Such reprises are frequent in the Rabbit novels, and they represent Harry's persisting sense of wonder that the world is just as it is and that he himself, just as *he* is, is always there to apprehend it. It is what makes him so often disappoint the people around him, and what reconciles them to him, however grudgingly; in his frequent incapacity for good works, he does "give them faith," though they seldom call it that.

*Rabbit, Run* is a tactfully religious novel whose spiritual implications are mostly proposed on the sly, by the not very authoritative Jack Eccles. One of the book's most terrifying moments is when Eccles's ameliorative, social-worker kind of ministry is challenged by a fire-breathing old Lutheran pastor: "'If Gott wants to end misery, He'll declare the Kingdom now.'" For the purposes of a religious novelist, that's much more like it, and *Rabbit Redux* shows that, a decade later, God has once again decided not to make that declaration just yet. In the meanwhile, Harry has returned to Janice and their son Nelson, lost track of Ruth, taken up his father's trade of linotyper, and bought a little tract house in a second-class suburb. His grim, inflexible mother is dying of Parkinson's disease, and Janice works at her father's used-car lot, recently adorned by a Toyota dealership, while (it emerges) carrying on an affair with Charlie Stavros, her father's best salesman. Around them all, the world is in 1969 quite visibly falling apart.

Though the religious questions raised by the earlier book continue as an undertone, *Rabbit Redux* is essentially a political novel of a particular historical moment. Its four sections bear epigraphs not from Pascal but from the subliminally bawdy technical talk of space exploration, and even in the hinterlands of Pennsylvania the abiding subjects are the moon shot, Vietnam, the morality of the rebellious young, and black revolution. Harry is an unabashed hawk on all such subjects, to the disgust of trendy Janice and her lover, a decent-minded liberal; but when Janice leaves him to live with Charlie, Harry wanders into the subworld of Brewer, from which he brings home Jill, a runaway young rich girl, and Skeeter, a bright, articulate, incorrigibly hostile young black drug dealer and racial messiah, to live with him and poor Nelson. With Jill he extends his sexual repertory; with Skeeter he samples the pleasures of illegal substances; with Nelson, who adores Jill and (for good reason) is terrified of Skeeter, he begins to enact the Oedipal conflict that will persist into *Rabbit Is Rich*. Jill dies when the neighbors, outraged at such carryings on, burn his house down, Skeeter takes his nihilistic faith into the wilderness, and Harry and Janice once again come back together to pick up the pieces of his lower being.

*Rabbit Redux* seems to me a flawed work, one of Updike's weaker novels, for several reasons. In it the pressure of history, which Updike was of course not alone in feeling in those difficult times, threatens to overpower the individuality of characters, who seem representative figures, spokesmen, rather than free dramatic agents. Jill and Skeeter are cartoons of the counterculture; Janice, Charlie, Nelson, and to a degree even Harry himself seem to have been assigned roles rather than permitted to have experiences (only Peggy Fosnacht, Janice's pathetic, overweight friend with whom Harry has a brief sexual interlude, seems to be fully alive); dialogue inclines toward debate, as in Harry's arguments with Charlie Stavros and Skeeter, where the voices speak less for any personal sense of things than for the public positions that everyone was arguing about at the end of the 1960s. As if aware of a danger, Updike made the book virtually a time capsule for 1969, stuffing it with current news stories, music, advertisements, and products; but the effect is of a theater in which the scenery is more vivid and authentic than the actors themselves. Certainly the book's catastrophe, Jill's violent destruction at the hands of bigots, belongs to a tradition of melodrama one had hoped Updike might disdain.

Both *Rabbit, Run* and *Rabbit Redux* end with images of feeling small and safe within large spaces, an acceptance by the microcosmic self of the macrocosmic "more." In *Rabbit, Run* Harry, in full flight from the entangling demands of domestic life, thinks "he doesn't know, what to do, where to go, what will happen, the thought that he doesn't know seems to make him infinitely small and impossible to capture. Its smallness fills him like a vastness," and in *Rabbit Redux*, in bed again with Janice like some Ulysses come home to Ithaca, "the space they are in, the motel room long and secret as a burrow, becomes all interior space" and he becomes, in effect, the "microscopic self" of his own penis. At the of *Rabbit Is Rich* the small object in a congenial space is not himself but the baby granddaughter in his arms; yet the new novel, however full of problems and anxieties, is governed by the mood of accepted security that its predecessors achieved only after long struggle.

If the first two Rabbit novels are religious and political, respectively, *Rabbit Is Rich* is clearly a story of the economic life. It leaps ahead another decade, to 1979, discovering an augmented Harry, both richer and fatter, in a depleted public reality. In a world which is running out of gas, he is cleaning up, managing his late father-in-law's Toyota agency and selling fuel-efficient cars like crazy. But death is present in this personal Arcadia, having taken not just Janice's father but both of Harry's parents and (he learns from a news clipping) the demonic Skeeter; and he senses its hand upon his mother-in-law; on the declining Charlie Stavros; on Thelma Murkett, with whom he has encyclopaedic sex when he and Janice try spouse-swapping on a Caribbean holiday with friends from the country club; on Peggy Fosnacht, who's had a breast removed; and even on himself, as he begins to feel worrisome twinges in the chest. Not too far away, Three Mile Island is behaving rather oddly.

Yet if disaster hovers around Harry and the nation generally, *Rabbit Is Rich* is a story of disasters averted. Updike teases us into anticipating tragedies that never quite occur: no one drowns or burns to death—no one, in fact, dies at all. Nelson's repeated fender-benders are never major accidents;

Harry's new daughter-in-law falls downstairs but does no lasting harm to herself or her unborn child; Nelson meets and is attracted to a girl who may be his illegitimate half-sister, the child Harry gave Ruth twenty years before, but they don't meet again and the threat of incest passes quietly. At the economic level, Harry's ignorant speculation in the rising gold and silver markets leads not to a wipe-out but to a decent gain; he sells too soon, but as they say on The Street, no one ever went bankrupt by taking a profit.

Harry's new prosperity is reflected in the quality of his domestic life. He and Janice have stayed together more or less happily for ten years. Their sex life is down a bit but still at least adequate; he still wishes she could cook oftener and better; they occasionally feel hampered by the presence of her mother, whose house they have shared since the fire in *Rabbit Redux*, but their existence is reasonably equable and contented. They have in fact moved toward the exurban good life of Updike's *Couples* and *Marry Me*, which for them centers upon the newish country club they've joined, with golf for him and tennis for her and, for both, considerable drinking with a small circle of fairly congenial friends of similar circumstances and outlooks.

This novel's disruptive force is not Harry or Janice but their son. Nelson is now twenty-three, an intermittent student at Kent State, where he has completed seven semesters in five years; at the beginning of the book he is in Colorado for the summer with a vaguely described girlfriend, hang-gliding and bumming around, but presently he shows up in Brewer with what seems to be quite a different girl, strangely determined to go into the automobile business with his father. Harry finds this an appalling prospect: he wants Nelson to finish college; he strongly doubts his business judgment (during his trial period Nelson takes a snowmobile as a trade-in and starts buying up old convertibles to sell as collectibles); he doesn't want to fire Charlie Stavros to make room for Nelson. But mostly he just doesn't want Nelson around, sensing (quite rightly) that the boy has both a specific hatred of his father for Jill's and his baby sister's deaths long ago and a more general and conventional desire, in effect, to destroy the father and take his place.

Though others keep assuring Harry that Nelson is very like him, the novel makes this seem true only in very limited ways. Nelson too is frightened by the demands of maturity and human obligation, and he too is a "runner," but both his behavior and Updike's occasional incursions into his consciousness reveal not Harry's hopeful interest in the terms of his own life but a cynical, surly, grasping, thoroughly stupid and unimaginative self-concern that is not like Harry at all. When a second girl (the first was a cover) shows up pregnant, Nelson recapitulates Harry's earlier career, insisting on marrying her against his father's advice, treating her quite badly, and deserting her three days before their child is born. But the parallels are formal only, author's contrivances; Nelson seems to me the one failure in *Rabbit Is Rich*, an irate caricature of the "Me Generation" where there might better be a difficult, confused, vulnerable human presence.

But elsewhere *Rabbit Is Rich* is a strong and secure novel, one of Updike's wisest and funniest. It is as full of the cultural details of 1979 as *Rabbit Redux* was full of those of 1969, but now such details are absorbed into the personal, private texture of Harry's experience. A lovely example is the scene where he and Janice, excited by dreams of speculative profit, make love on a bed heaped with newly-bought Krugerrands. (One coin gets lost in the turmoil, but in this novel nothing is irretrievably lost, and it turns up between the mattress and the bedframe.) The effect is not some simple irony about confusion or displacement of desires—they make love not to but *through* the gold, treating the things of this world not as objects but as a medium through which to approach "a more." The incident echoes Harry's fantasy in *Rabbit, Run*, when, fleeing from marriage for the first time, he sees a road sign for Wilmington and "wonders what it's like to make it to a Du Pont," a conjunction of monetary and sexual possession he repeats near the end of *Rabbit Is Rich*, flying in a jet over Delaware. Like other things in the Rabbit novels, this owes something to Joyce's *Ulysses*—Harry's covetous image of well-booted Du Pont girls flicking their riding crops is in touch with the more passive fancies of another "plebian Don Juan," Leopold Bloom, about high-society Amazons like The Honourable Mrs. Mervyn Talboys. But Harry's version fits into his own cultural geography as neatly as does Updike's delighted perception of how well a famous advertising slogan—"YOU ASKED FOR IT, WE GOT IT"—suits the combination of irrepressible randiness and an almost saintly capacity for sympathy and concern in this particular Toyota dealer.

*Rabbit Is Rich* is the quietest, mellowest—without derogation, the most middle-aged—of the Harry Angstrom novels. Updike's famous, rather dangerous powers of style remain under control, small domestic details are trusted to generate and direct action that earlier depended upon larger and more theatrical devices. Here a remarkable literary talent, far from running out of gas, rides smoothly and efficiently in overdrive, getting maximum mileage from minimal apparent effort. Harry himself is in some ways diminished in his middle age; his acceptance of affluence and domestication may mark a falling off of his faith in his own uniqueness, "his sense," as he describes it to Thelma, his newest lover, "of miracle at being himself, himself instead of somebody else, and his old inkling, now fading in the energy crunch, that there was something that wanted him to find it out, that he was here on earth on a sacred assignment." But this is also a story of new beginnings, however modest their possibilities—a fine new Celica loaded with options and "charisma"; an elegant little stone house in, at last, the best suburb; hints that Nelson may finish college and come home to his new family and that he may not be quite as hopeless at business as Harry has feared (the convertibles and even the snowmobile do in fact sell); and above all a new granddaughter to engage the feelings the long-dead daughter and the lost son are no longer there to receive.

Imagining a life like Harry Angstrom's brings into play Updike's strongest fictional gifts, the gifts that function intermittently in *The Centaur* and are radiantly clear in the Olinger stories and *Of The Farm*. One of these gifts is an illusionless but tender understanding of how families work, how husbands and wives, parents and children, in the name of love and obligation, do unforgiveable things to one another and yet may, in the mysteriousness of their felt bonds, achieve some measure or form of forgiveness. Another is a sense of the sanctity of memory, the mind's power to preserve and in a way redeem a life of errors and losses. Harry, in effect, remembers everything: new experience acquires its meaning by becoming, in his mind, a celebration of, or an elegy for, something past, a process of "recollection" in which nothing is ever truly lost.

And, I would suppose, Harry matters to Updike because in imagining his fictional character the novelist also honors the memory of his own origins. Harry is almost exactly Updike's own age, and the "Brewer" of the novels pointedly resembles the area around Reading where Updike grew up. Updike of course went off to Harvard, Oxford, *The New Yorker*, and literary stardom, while Harry never even went to college but instead was drafted, got married, and slowly and unsteadily proceeded to a much more modest success. Harry is a kind of Updikeian anti-self, derived from the envy, and pity, which bright and verbal kids feel for ones whose gifts are mainly physical, the adolescent trope of athleticism and sexuality that the mature male psyche never quite outgrows. By now, the two men have little in common except vigorous erotic imaginations and a liking for golf, but in Harry Updike continues to explore and ponder his own beginnings and where they might have led. Such material, with its sobering depth of feeling, is good for a writer whose seriousness is continually dogged by the shadow of his own marvelous facility.

It seems quite possible that we will get another Rabbit novel around 1990—*Rabbit is Ruined? Rabbit Raffiné?* But as Dante knew, three is a useful number, and a Rabbit trilogy, should it turn out to be that, would do nicely for a kind of *Commedia* of the ordinary life in modern America.

# DEMOCRATIC VISTAS

*The next two items have a buried connection in the theme of difficult American renewal in a period—the Reagan years—when easy renewals were much more talked about. Peter Davis and Richard Reeves were looking for what (at his own level of understanding) Ronald Reagan hoped to find too, an America that retained some of the shape and feel of Tocquevillian democracy before it was compromised by modern decadence. In* The Mosquito Coast *Paul Theroux reimagined a quintessential American type—the practical idealist, the dreaming mechanic-artificer—driven from home by his vision of an adequate freedom, only to find that it isn't available anywhere; but Allie Fox's bemused son Charlie, another American type—the pragmatic adaptor, like Huck Finn or Melville's Ishmael—survives, as if to suggest that renewal isn't wholly out of the question, if we don't insist on having too much of it all at once.*

# Good Morning, America
(1982)

*I*T'S not often spelled with a "k" these days, and after two decades of doubt and disaffection many people seem able to hope that "America" is no longer a dirty word. In writing about the state of the nation neither Peter Davis nor Richard Reeves adopts the mood of our present rulers, but both cautiously assume a continuity in the American character that would not dismay Ronald Reagan.

To most of us the 1960s and 1970s seemed endless, and indeed they comprised a good tenth of our national existence. It was as if the collective American self during those years was enduring something like what overprivileged young men and women have to endure between the ages (roughly) of fifteen to seventeen: the first strong emergence of, and resistance to, adult consciousness, with its unwelcome discovery that what one does and says has consequences for oneself and for other people, that the sources that have fed one's desires are not limitless, that one must work for, or appear to be working for, at least some of what one hopes to get or keep. Having learned the hard way that we are no better or brighter than the rest of the world, Americans now face a kind of self-examination different from the older uncertainties, so amusing to foreign observers, of a people without history, tradition, or intelligible style.

Peter Davis, a successful and serious-minded television and film producer (*Hearts and Minds, The Selling of the Pentagon, Middletown*), approaches the present condition of America as if making a documentary. *Hometown* portrays a small midwestern city, Hamilton, Ohio, in ways that would work well on screen—he shows us a lower-middle-class wedding, a basketball game between the town's "good" (mostly white) and "bad" (racially mixed) high schools, a strike at a local tool factory, a comparison of a fundamentalist minister with a police-court judge as dispensers of "justice," a virtually stenographic rendering of the gossip at a beauty shop, and so on. The continuing theme is tension, the disparity between hopeful public surfaces and the personal and social antagonisms they mask.

Davis explains, in the rhetoric of "serious" television, that his purpose was to "map the passions of one American town," and, wanting to do things right, he first asked a government demographer where to look for some mappable passions:

> Tell me where I can go to combine categories of social research with techniques of storytelling. Where I can observe activities the way an anthropologist might, as Robert and Helen Lynd did in *Middletown*, and then tell about them as Sherwood Anderson did in *Winesburg, Ohio*. Stories of marriage and morals, work and leisure, politics, crime, punishment, religion, caste and class. Stories of real people using not only fact but fantasy, not only information but impression, attitude, legend—diverse tidings that disclose particular truths in a community.

Davis doesn't put this in quotation marks, and I suspect he didn't really make his request with such guileless pomposity. But more than style is a problem here. The stories he found in

Hamilton are precisely the ones he was looking for—and it was tough luck on Hamilton that he chose to find them *there*.

Worse, his hope of "using not only fact but fantasy" encourages a suspicious reader to look for some rigging. One of the book's two central episodes, both juicy crime stories, develops out of a description of a particular policeman's shift of duty on a particular (but undated) evening. Although Davis never says outright that he was riding with Sergeant Chuck Furman on the night in question, he reports Furman's rounds very circumstantially, and since he also records Furman's comments on various criminals to someone else who seems to be in the car, it becomes easy to assume that Davis himself was there, on that night.

As it happens, Furman is called (at 11:11 PM) to respond to a reported "shooting involving two white males at 2132 North K Street." At that moment Furman and his putative interviewer-passenger vanish from the narrative, which moves into a long account of the events leading up to what turns out to be a sensational murder case, one which according to Davis epitomizes the unequal distribution of human opportunities in Hamilton and America. In watching TV or a movie, of course, we know that a good deal of cutting and splicing is implied in what we see; but readers of a narrative in print may want to ask some questions. Did Davis just happen to be in Hamilton, on the right night, in that police car, when such a useful crime offered itself? If so, he was remarkably lucky, especially since the circumstances so happily suited his sociological purposes. Or did the murder take place before he went to Hamilton (he was clearly at the trial, but that's easier to manage), so that he had in effect to provide an establishing sequence, by (perhaps) riding with Furman at some later time and weaving in details from the dispatcher's log for the murder night? Whatever the case, a reader may want to know what is "a dramatization" and what Davis directly witnessed.

This is not a major objection—the story of this crime and its punishment is instructive and troubling however it is presented. But in *Hometown* Davis's concern for the cinematographic necessities of dramatic immediacy competes with his social and moral seriousness. He came to Hamilton, he tells us, because the demographer recommended it as representative—big enough yet small enough, Northern (industrial) and Southern (rural) and Western (once on the frontier) and Eastern (with enough of a history) all at once. Hamilton is asked to be all America, and that's too much for any one town to be. And the evidence Davis looks for is highly representative—class conflict between the indigenous industrial bosses and the newcomers (Appalachian whites, blacks) who now do most of the work; the high incidence of divorce just as in California or New York; the decline of public school enrollments and of population generally in the old industrial cities; the renascence of Protestant extremism, all those disturbing problems that are worried about on serious talk shows.

They of course *are* disturbing problems, and Hamilton, Ohio, no doubt has its share of them. But Davis's way of merging social research and storytelling creates problems of its own. The vivid presence and telling juxtaposition on which the filmmaker's imagination thrives cause noticeable strain, as when he tries to make modern Hamilton's interest in the rumored sexual peccancies of its handsome young mayor seem parallel to the town's excitement in the 1820s about the struggles of a local hollow-earther, one John Cleves Symmes, to win international recognition for his Theory of Polar Voids. The connection eludes analysis, and others proposed in the book are at least a little frail. And Davis the storyteller is too receptive to the dramatic possibilities of the lurid—the gossip about the charismatic mayor and his dismaying death, the murder case, the bitter conflict over the school board's efforts to dismiss a music teacher accused of exposing himself in a department-store men's room—to leave enough space for the soberer modes of social research.

It seems curious that Davis, himself so indebted to the techniques of television and movies, should display what seems to be a conventional moral and perhaps political dislike of them. Though he allows that TV, because it "has no will of its own," can't be a *directly* bad influence on us, he seems pleased to remark of the murder case that "it would be hard to imagine a crime to which television was more intimately connected," since it hinged on a separated couple's dispute over who would get the TV set and since the killer would not have encountered his victim on the fatal night if he hadn't got bored with watching a baseball game. (Insufficient evidence, since it would be hard to imagine *any* domestic event in America without a TV somewhere in the picture.)

The *Today* show is twitted for doing a laudatory segment on a "back to basics" movement in the Hamilton schools without saying or even knowing that the superintendent whom they interviewed on camera was then leading a vendetta against an allegedly homosexual teacher. The local paper's candor, which some Hamiltonians thought smutty, in quoting words like "erection" and "masturbation" from the testimony in that case is explained: "In its vividness, the *Journal-News* was possibly grafting another species of writing onto responsible journalism, adapting an alien form to new uses. But it was not pornography, only screenplay." This sounds like irony, but its target isn't clear—"responsible journalism"? prudery? or just screen-writing? But I know where I am when Davis, in one of his social-protest moods, calls television one of "the tranquilizers of the poor," though I wonder if he thinks the rich never watch it.

*Hometown* has its virtues. Davis can be a good observer

and listener, and he is fair-minded. He gives, for example, a surprisingly complex and sympathetic portrait of "Boss" Beckett, a back-country aristocrat who is the town's leading citizen, and reality cooperates nicely when Beckett, a reactionary on social and economic issues, affirms his personal decency by siding, against most of his peers as well as some of the local liberals, with the poor teacher the school board wants to fire. There are other good things in the book, enough to make me wish all the more that Davis hadn't been so eager to make Hamilton an image of America and to apprehend its life in ways that would play well on the screen.

While Davis strongly dislikes much that Hamilton and America now contain, he does offer some cheer. We are not so different from our ancestors, he suggests magniloquently:

> Blinded by speed, inventions, new means of transportation, we focus on change to the exclusion of permanence. What generation since the founding of the Republic has not thought itself living in transition, has not longed for the time when children obeyed, a dollar was worth a dollar, the boss knew all his workers by their first names? It is hard to escape the conclusion that permanence, continuity, relative fixity are paid insufficient attention in a society that, even when fearful of it, reveres and generally profits from change. In thrall to the gospel of change, we overlook what is continuous; one of the most enduring features of the American landscape is change itself.

Some of these continuities are of course pretty discreditable; Davis has in fact just been quoting a nineteenth-century Hamiltonian orator who praised his pioneer forebears for being not idealists or reformers but "practical eradicationists" who understood that "the most certain road to successful competition with savage man and beast was to exterminate them." But invoking "permanence" is philosophically bracing, the touch of uplift that cushions bad news, and it can be as useful to a journalist like Richard Reeves as it is to Davis.

"Traveling with Tocqueville in Search of *Democracy in America*," the subtitle of Reeves's *American Journey*, sounds encouraging. What better guide to present complexity than that astute, entertaining Frenchman who long ago defined our character and institutions so enduringly? Reeves undertakes to celebrate the sesquicentennial of Tocqueville's American visit by retracing his route and comparing our America with his.

This is a pleasant idea, if perhaps a risky one for a long book—it is not meant as an insult to say that the more he gives us of Tocqueville, the less attention we pay to Reeves. Following Tocqueville geographically is sometimes awkward for him, too. He starts at Newport, Rhode Island, simply because Tocqueville did so; but Reeves can't find much to say about Newport except that there's a lot of information in the air there—seventy-nine radio and eight television stations are receivable, not to mention a store that sells 250 different magazines. This states an important if not very fresh fact about America, but it doesn't distinguish Newport from Council Bluffs or Fresno.

Reeves shares both Davis's conviction that "America" is everywhere you look and Davis's way of uttering that conviction with a rise of the voice that for my generation eternally evokes *Life* magazine, *The March of Time*, and the estimable Edward R. Murrow. Reeves tells us he has been living in California and first thought of doing a Tocqueville out West:

> But, soon enough, I learned that the questions and the themes—mine and Tocqueville's—were the same everywhere in the great land. . . . We were, I found, one people: Americans. There were no regional answers to

questions of war and peace, of equality, of justice. The question was still American democracy: What had it become? Did it work? Could it peacefully translate the will of the people into life, liberty, and the pursuit of happiness for each of those people?

This is an odd way for a tough-minded reporter to be talking, especially if he's been reading the witty and illusionless Tocqueville, but I suppose it shows the reviving power of words like "America" and "democracy" to turn thought into rubber. Like his great model, Reeves seeks a panoramic view of American attitudes and institutions, and the present scene strikes him as at least as ambiguous and uncompleted as America seemed to Tocqueville. *American Journey* is a kind of anthology of our difficulties, challenges, and follies. At his best Reeves is a smart and diligent journalist, and he is better than most when he writes on the press and television, on the behavior of political and economic leaders, the condition of racial minorities and women, the changing modes of work and worship and leisure.

Some of his details are splendidly sharp. Invited in New York to dine with Mayor Koch, he finds that the other guests are the mayor's subordinates or cronies, all bent on self-congratulation just as their counterparts were when Mayor Walter Bowne had Tocqueville to dinner in 1831. ("These people seem to me stinking with national conceit," Tocqueville wrote to his mother.) Thinking about corporate agglomeration in the information business, Reeves reflects that Tocqueville's itinerary now would permit him to read twenty-eight Gannett newspapers and wonders how that might affect the power of a free press, which Tocqueville found so impressive, to counter governmental oppression. When told by Reeves of a fanatical right-wing evangelist he's heard on local radio, an eminent Louisville newspaper publisher says, "I don't know why they allow things like that on the air," evidently forgetting that, as Reeves later learned, his family's corporation owns the station in question.

Tocqueville's presence in the narrative is consistently useful. In Nashville, pondering the popular music industry, Reeves wickedly recalls what Tocqueville wrote when *he* heard America singing: "We spend our life enduring howling of which one has no conception in the old world." At a very different level, the comment of Felix Rohatyn on a grave present concern—"The treatment of poor blacks is the test of our democracy. . . . Democracy may be a great luxury that works only so long as there is growth to allocate. The system still hasn't been tested in allocating sacrifice. Will the middle class sacrifice to keep black mothers on welfare? I don't think so."— reminds us of Tocqueville's warning that "the most formidable evil threatening the future of the United States is the presence of the blacks on their soil."

Tocqueville's wondering discovery that American democracy undertook to offer Americans "a continuous and unending amelioration of social conditions" is grotesquely fulfilled in Reeves's story about a private club in Saginaw, Michigan which had to close its squash courts because, in violation of federal and state regulations, the doors were too small to allow access to people in wheelchairs. Reeves's sober account of present-day feminism gains amusing historical point in Tocqueville's amazement at how docilely American wives ("those charming recluses") submerged their being within their mates'—"the eldorado of husbands," he called America in a teasing letter to his sister-in-law.

But even Tocqueville can't quite make *American Journey* what Reeves wants it to be. For all his shrewd comment, his subjects remain the staples of serious popular journalism, and his tireless interrogation of witnesses causes a problem of focus. The people whose views he records, however questioningly, are mainly the system's top-dogs, not those who have to cope with it from within or below. Visiting the prison at Auburn, New York, he accumulates facts (it costs $9,736 a year to maintain a prisoner, for example) and offers a theory of not much interest (that prisons are a little like universities), but while he quotes one prisoner, who says it's *dangerous* in there, his conception of the place comes mostly from interviewing the warden.

His main sources are business executives, publishers and editors, political leaders, professors, lawyers, and financiers, as if the country were a comic-opera army with more generals than privates. He of course doesn't believe all he hears from these sources, and I can see that when you come to an unfamiliar place, you naturally seek help from those who know how it works, who are usually the people in charge. But he describes the anatomy of old power facing new challenges, his major subject, in the vocabulary of the overclass, and the very presence of that vocabulary keeps us from seeing things from other perspectives, the kinds that Oscar Lewis or Robert Coles or Studs Terkel or for that matter Peter Davis (who's very good on how Hamilton's ordinary people talk and feel) could provide.

*American Journey*, like *Hometown*, is weakened by arbitrariness, by being too quick to treat observations as metaphors for the list of Big Subjects the observer brought along with him. Reeves knows what items belong on any such list in the 1980s: the shift of population and economic strength from Tocqueville's part of America to parts south and west; the domination of local life and work by distant powers—the national government, big labor, agglomerated business, and homogenized information and entertainment; the dangers of entrusting the productive mechanisms to the bottom-line mentality of accountants and lawyers, instead of to those who can make and sell usable goods; the shift from treating work as a measure of personal value and a means of offering future opportunity to one's descendants—and, through them, to the community and the nation—to treating it as support for a "life-style," with "freedom" increasingly coming to mean "free time"; the frightening prospects for poor people in a system that may not be willing or able to pay for justice or even decency much longer. Such subjects need all the attention they can get, but their urgency isn't fully served by Reeves's rather loose ways of attaching some of them to the places he visits, or by his continual appeal to voices from afar—the experts he's consulted in Washington, New York, Cambridge, or wherever—to tell him what's really happening out there in humbler parts of the Republic.

In an important sense, as Reeves and Davis say, we are of course one people, figures in an intellectual and moral intention, "democracy," which most of us, routinely or thoughtfully, accept and value. As usual, Tocqueville explains that intention better than anyone else. First he asks us to be clear about what we want from society and government. Do we want them to raise us to "an elevated and generous view of the things of this world," "a certain scorn of material goods," in order to improve manners, foster "poetry, renown, and glory," achieve "powerful influence over all others," attempt "great enterprises" and leave "a great mark on history"? If so, we should not support democratic government.

> But if you think it profitable to turn man's intellectual and moral activity toward the necessities of physical life and use them to produce well-being, if you think that reason is more use to men than genius, if your object is not to create heroic virtues but rather tranquil habits, if you would rather contemplate vices than crimes and prefer fewer transgressions at the cost of

fewer splendid deeds, if in place of a brilliant society you are content to live in one that is prosperous, and finally, if in your view the main object of government is not to achieve the greatest strength or glory for the nation as a whole but to provide for every individual therein the utmost well-being, protecting him as far as possible from all afflictions, then it is good to make conditions equal and to establish a democratic government.

For Tocqueville's neoclassical mind, the choice is in effect between epic and pastoral, and in the necessary messiness of practice, choices are not quite so clear. But his words suggest how far two decades of imperial presidencies have taken us from the moral center of what American democracy originally had in mind. The philosophical and economic incompatibility of national "reason" and national "genius" are only too evident in the cross-purposes of Reaganism, and of most of those who oppose it as well.

To the extent that *Hometown* and *American Journey* depart from the conventions of upbeat popular journalism and look closely enough to see America as caught in a confusion of aims that may be inescapable, they are both worth reading. But finally the "America" they consider seems an abstraction, and it comes as something of a relief to realize that we are *not*, or at least not yet, one people, that our diversities of class, religion, region, ethnicity, sex, and personal taste remain more strange and interesting than either writer admits. The large questions are not the only ones, or necessarily the most important ones, to be asked about American life now. Perhaps it's that both authors are "coastal" people—Reeves born in Jersey City, trained in New York, living in California, and Davis born in California, living in New York, and (presumably) working in both places—but whatever the reason, I feel sure that Hamilton, Ohio, is much more (if not inevitably much better) than Davis's verbal cinema can show, and that the places Reeves visited must feel, to most of their inhabitants, rather different from what he heard from their potentates. This is good to remember in times as bad as these, as it is always good to remember how much of life eludes the categories we try to apply to it. Both writers, to their credit, are at least trying to think seriously about America within the customs of their crafts. It's just that, as usual, so much remains to be said.

# Crackpot Crusoe
(1982)

THOUGH Paul Theroux commands language with fine intelligence and grace, some may wonder whether his writing is much more than sophisticated entertainment. His novels openly have predecessors, other books whose terms they appropriate and exploit; and these predecessors, though often considerable, aren't always the really "major" work we expect an ambitious young writer to emulate. In *The Family Arsenal* the Conrad of *The Secret Agent* consorts with early Graham Greene and tough American detective stories; *The Black House* plays with the stuff of popular domestic Gothic; *Saint Jack* and *The Consul's File* draw upon an Anglo-colonial fiction that includes Maugham and Kipling as well as Forster, Orwell, and the younger Anthony Burgess. Can so dependent and eclectic a talent be important?

My belief that Theroux's talent is indeed important is strengthened by *The Mosquito Coast*. Here again predecessors are abundantly evident. *Robinson Crusoe, The Swiss Family Robinson, Heart of Darkness, Lord of the Flies, Walden, Moby Dick, Huckleberry Finn*—the list is almost scandalous. They come together, however, not as a pastiche but in a strong and disturbing fable that illuminates the literature it draws upon even as it finds its own imaginative integrity.

*The Mosquito Coast* is the story of a Yankee genius, Allie Fox, a Maine-born Harvard drop-out, a self-taught engineer and inventor with a number of patents to his credit, a rejector of God and the American Way and all other sources of poor workmanship, a born counterculturalist and survivalist who feels nothing but scorn for such canting creeds. In the beginning, Fox lives in Hatfield, Massachusetts, with his patient wife and four children, doing odd jobs for Tiny Polski, an avaricious but not wholly unamiable asparagus grower, and trying to fend off an America of fast foods, television, drugs, crime, pollution, pornography, religious fanaticism, and cheap imports. His interest in the Central American migrant workers whom Polski exploits leads him to a great decision: to pack up his family and seek a new life in the jungles of Honduras.

In his rejection of America, Fox is of course a classic American type, and his will to create a new and better reality ("There's a whole world out there!," he hopefully cries) would be understood at Brook Farm or Walden Pond or any frontier homestead. At Jeronimo, an overgrown clearing in remote upriver Honduras, he magisterially creates his imagined better world, where crops flourish, sound houses rise, water is easily pumped to bath-house, latrine, and laundry, old bicycles become self-propelled boats, and so on.

"Father" (as even the puzzled but entranced natives call Fox) is, by his own account, a kind of Industrial Darwinist, a comber of beaches and dumps for materials whose value only he understands:

> "The things that get to this beach are indestructible remnants that survived the storms and tides and the bite of the sea. They've proved themselves—stood the test of weather and time. By putting them to use, we

# Crackpot Crusoe 165

are making a settlement that can't be destroyed. Your average Crusoe castaway lives like a monkey. But I'm no fool. Take these toilet seats. That's natural selection. The hoppers are gone, but they're everlasting."

But if Father's theories are shaky ("hoppers" are not more destructible than toilet seats, they just don't *float*), his practice is astonishingly effective; as the centerpiece of his new creation, this inspired *bricoleur* constructs his master-work, a gigantic edifice of old pipes and boilerplate which, in effect, transforms fire into ice.

In (evidently) a consciously sardonic conflating of the nicknames of the Hiroshima and Nagasaki bombs, Father calls his ice-maker "Fat Boy," and the project neatly expresses the heroic contradictions within his imagination—what more magnificent and yet futile gift for the people of tropical jungles than free ice? The ice does tend to melt before it can be delivered, but for Father it's a strong demonstration of his power to create virtually *ex nihilo*. Needless to say, he's desolated when supposedly aboriginal tribesmen recognize it as "hice" and honor it by reciting the Lord's Prayer in only somewhat garbled English.

God is of course Father's great problem. If He ever did exist, He badly botched the job of Creation, and Father himself must do it over. But even in the wilderness there are humiliating evidences of a prior creation. Sanctimonious missionaries meddle with Father's designs. Place names like "Guampu" rub shoulders with ones like "Mobilgasna." In "the hottest, dirtiest, nastiest corner of Honduras" Father comes upon a corroded flashlight battery. Deep in the bush a missionary family watches the Muppets and plays Space Invaders on their cassette TV while eating ice cream from their freezer. As Father seeks an unfallen realm commensurate with his creative powers, his own children construct a refuge in a hidden glade, where with the native kids they play at buying and selling, going to church and making phone calls, just as God meant us to do.

Fox has apparently spent some time in a mental hospital, and in Honduras his initially charming eccentricity turns increasingly paranoid and megalomaniac. At its best, his is the harmless nuttiness of the village explainer who's utterly oblivious of his audience, as in his insistence that engineering is just anatomy writ large:

> "Insulation? Look at fatty tissue!" You had to study natural things. Anyone who took a good look at an alligator or a hicatee could make an armored vehicle. The natural world showed man what was possible. In a world without birds there would be no airplanes. "Airplanes are just magnified sparrows—they're crascos with leg room."
>
> The Zambus stared at Father, and the others listened twitchily to this man who the harder he worked the more he talked.
>
> "What's a savage?" he said. "It's someone who doesn't bother to look around and see that he can change the world."
>
> Everyone looked around and said this was so.

But Fox's demand for a reality of his own shaping takes increasingly darker forms. He refuses to join his family in learning to use natural foods and medicines—nature unimproved by his mind is unacceptable; he imposes cruel tests and punishments upon his rebellious sons; he grows intellectually dishonest, insisting that each failure of his designs is in fact part of his plan. Most insanely, in his obsession with the collapse of

American culture, he becomes convinced that in his absence the United States has been destroyed by nuclear holocaust, so that his own reality is the only one left.

Theroux clearly admires Fox's very American refusal to settle for less than his mind can conceive, but he also acknowledges an equally American anxiety about imaginative hubris. Fox's frenzy of inventive construction exemplifies what Richard Poirier, in *A World Elsewhere*, identified as a central trope of American literature, "building" conceived as an expansion of self in order to possess an environment that would otherwise remain nature's (or God's) alone, a substitution of self for world. This substitution, however, "is possible only if the imagination and space are freed from the possessive power of all that is not nature: from systems of any kind that derive from society and history, from, often as not, 'Europe.'"

It is both a heroic effort and a futile one, futile, at least, from the perspective of narrators like Melville's Ishmael or Fitzgerald's Nick Carraway, surrogates for readers who are perforce a part of that prior world of "systems" and who remain, however reluctantly, to prove its persistence after the story itself is over. In *The Mosquito Coast* the narrator-surrogate is Fox's older son, Charlie, a young teen-ager who admires, resents, and fears his remarkable father. In Massachusetts he wishes that Father (who despises mass education) would let him go to school like the other kids; in Honduras, for all his pride in Father's miracles, he yearns to go back home and be ordinary. But if Theroux shares some of Fox's dislike for what Charlie's conformity desires, he also sees the useful strength of conformity, which at least permits Charlie to resist, and survive, the extremity of his father's demands upon life.

Charlie's unsophisticated perceptiveness, like Huck Finn's, gives his author room for uninsistent ironic maneuverings. It is Charlie, for example, when compelled by Father to climb to the top of Fat Boy, who in the midst of his terror notices that the device somehow resembles Father's body and particularly, in its upper reaches, his head; and it is Charlie who near the end, when Father's body lies grievously wounded ("I can't get out of this thing," he touchingly complains) reflects that his head is the only part of him still alive. Charlie doesn't connect these moments or comment on what they might say about mind's risky involvement with world, but through him Theroux suggests implications that would be less troubling if the narrator were consciously in control of them.

Charlie, who lights out not for The Territory but back to the safety of teen-age America, is finally not Huck Finn. But his painful need both to admire and reject his imposing father corresponds to the mixed feelings American readers may have about so essentially American a figure as Allie Fox. Fox's literary origins are of course European and romantic, deriving from the intransigent "madness" of writers like (as Yeats put it) "that William Blake / Who beat upon the wall / Till Truth obeyed his call." But for us Fox is closer to Cooper's Deerslayer, Melville's Ahab, the fabulous artificers of Poe and Hawthorne, and also to the Wizard of Oz and that mighty line, from Franklin through Edison and the Wrights to Buckminster Fuller, of real-life crackpots who knew more than we thought. How are we to feel about a modern American heroic builder who must try to free his imagination not from an idea of "Europe" but from an all too real America whose creation, in a terrible and unsuspected way, was adumbrated in the great American fictions of freedom and self-expansion from which a figure like Allie Fox draws his literary being? Can there be an American hero, an "American novel" in the old sense of opposition to prior cultural authority, in a world where "America" more and more seems to be the name for all that there is?

Theroux's book doesn't force us into these rather deep waters; it is a fine entertainment, a strong adventure story, a remarkable comic portrayal of minds and cultures at cross-purposes. But *The Mosquito Coast*, under its unintimidating surface, shows an expatriate novelist seriously reflecting upon his sources, as an American writer and an American, and the difficult relations of those sources to the world as it now seems to be.

# A SENSE OF THE PAST

*Not renewal but the wreckage of the American consciousness is the theme of the next two pieces. Both Joan Didion and Neil Postman saw in us a nation ruined by its history—for Didion, the hypocrisies and evasions of American imperium, for Postman the corruption of our taste and judgement by television. Rather than Tocqueville, the governing presences are (for Didion) Henry Adams and (for Postman) Marshall McLuhan. I found Didion's novel successful and Postman's cultural critique unconvincing, which may be to say that the message is not inevitably the medium.*

# *The American Exemption*
(1984)

JOAN Didion is one of those writers—Norman Mailer, Mary McCarthy, and Gore Vidal are others—who are so good at the higher journalism that their status as novelists may sometimes seem insecure. Do they, we may wonder, keep writing fiction out of professional pride, as if only the novel could truly certify their literary talent and seriousness? Are not their novels, however fine, shadowed by a suspicion, however baseless, that the form isn't quite the best package for such powers?

Certainly Didion's *Democracy* opens with an ominous display of skepticism about the moves required of it as fictional narrative:

> The light at dawn during those Pacific tests was something to see.
> Something to behold.
> Something that could almost make you think you saw God, he said.
> He said to her.
> Jack Lovett said to Inez Victor.
> Inez Victor who was born Inez Christian.

Such self-revising fumbling with the identity cards that novels are supposed to slip quietly under the door seems a little like having the magician confess that the rabbit came out of his vest and not the empty topper. "This is a hard story to tell," complains the last sentence of this first chapter, and the manner of opening makes you wonder if for Didion the old game is still worth playing.

Yet what we have here does seem to be a "chapter"—it began with a "1" and after some blank space and the turn of a page we find a new block of print headed "2." Despite the authorial shufflings, a story begins to get told, as if impelled by the stubborn insistencies of narrative itself, the odd necessity of continuing once you have, for whatever reason, started. The signs of anti-fiction don't disappear, to be sure. "Call me the author," the second chapter begins, followed by a glimpse of a writer named "Joan Didion"—done in the manner not of Melville but, of all people, Trollope—who is struggling to get her story going:

> Consider any of these things long enough and you will see that they tend to deny the relevance not only of personality but of narrative, which makes them less than ideal images with which to begin a novel, but we go with what we have.

So indeed we do, but counter-illusion has begun to generate its own, second-order kind of credence. If this narrator is *the* Joan Didion, the one who went to Berkeley, worked for *Vogue* in 1960, now lives in Los Angeles but travels to far-off places as a journalist, and so on, then Inez Victor and Jack Lovett and the other people in this book may be real too, since Joan Didion says she knew them. Maybe she does have nothing up her sleeve.

For a critic this is good fun, but most readers of novels want the puppets to come to life, and in *Democracy* they tend to do so before long, despite the author's resistences. Inez Victor, we hear and want to believe, is a child of privilege. She was born in 1935, in Hawaii, to a mainland girl from Stockton who did some modeling at Magnin's in San Francisco before she was swept off her feet and over the seas by Paul Christian, the footloose and increasingly odd son of one of those rich old families whose economic conquest of the Islands was an early if somewhat benign instance of Yankee colonialism. As Didion pieces together Inez's story, we learn that she went to Sarah Lawrence, married (when two months pregnant) an ambitious young lawyer named Harry Victor, bore twins, worked in New York with Joan Didion, and then settled, uncomfortably, into the quasi-public role of political wife.

Harry Victor, with his keen eye for the main chance, became an activist lawyer in the sixties, got himself elected to Congress and then the Senate, came close to winning a presidential nomination in 1972, and now devotes himself to something called the Alliance for Democratic Institutions. He's an odious man, full of a liberal self-importance that views the world and himself in it as "incorporeal extensions of policy," over-responsive to the young women who swarm around him and his causes (one of them, a pop singer, is charmingly modest about her talents—"I just do two lines of coke and scream"), deeply attached to his own untested slogans and to the joys of radical chic. He's virtually a cartoon, but Didion allows him just enough human shading to suggest, in case we hadn't noticed, how cartoon-like media politics really is.

Harry is less successful as paterfamilias than as public image. His son, the marvelously named Adlai, is a pompous lunkhead who barely gets into an obscure college near Boston but likes to talk grandly about what's what "in Cambridge." Adlai's twin, Jessie, equally dumb but sweeter, becomes a heroin addict in prep school not out of rebellion or despair but simply as a "consumer decision." Sent off to Seattle for methadone and work therapy, she makes her way to Saigon just as the last Americans are being evacuated, because someone told her you could find interesting jobs there.

Inez deals with her marriage by dying a little inside. She comes to consider "most occasions as photo opportunities;" she works dutifully for good causes and is rumored to have a drinking problem; she reflects that she's been "most happy in borrowed houses, and at lunch." Asked by a reporter what the greatest cost of public life is, she answers "memory, mostly," and when urged to explain, she simply says "you lose track." It seems an acute comment on why presidential advisors and others close to power seem so surprised that discrepencies in the record bother other people so seriously—having to say and do so much just to hold your audience, you cease to care about, and then even to remember, what really happened or what you said about it at the time.

The devastating personal and public consequences of the loss of history are Didion's theme. The significant relations between events wash away in a flood of mere information, all those details which, because equally circumstantial, news reporting democratically represents as being about equal in import:

> I would skim the stories on policy and fix instead on details: the cost of a visa to leave Cambodia in the weeks before Phnom Penh closed was five hundred dollars American. The colors of the landing lights for the helicopters on the roof of the American embassy in Saigon were red, white, and blue. The code names for the American evacuations of Cambodia and Vietnam respectively were EAGLE PULL and FREQUENT WIND. The amount of cash burned in the courtyard of the DAO in Saigon before the last helicopter left was three-and-a-half million dollars American and eighty-five million piastres. The code name for this operation

was MONEY BURN. The number of Vietnamese soldiers who managed to get aboard the last American 727 to leave Da Nang was three hundred and thirty. The number of Vietnamese soldiers to drop from the wheel wells of the 727 was one. The name of the pilot was Ken Healy.

The voice here is Joan Didion's, not Inez Victor's, but the malady it reflects is Inez's and of course our own too. Vietnam is the most dramatic recent evidence of where the appetite for power can lead democracy, but the larger subject is the evanescence of thought and moral awareness in a swirl of endlessly unsortable information.

It is the reading of this particular news story, on March 26, 1975, that leads Joan Didion to another news story, a report of what becomes the decisive event of Inez Victor's life. This is the murder in Honolulu, by Inez's now-insane father, of her sister Janet and Wendell Omura, a local anti-war congressman who may have been Janet's lover. This violent conjunction of racial and familial motives merges private tragedy into public disaster; it leads Inez toward something like freedom and the novel toward a justification of its intricate method, in what seems to me its most impressive stroke of political imagination.

The temporal circlings of Didion's narrative began, if just barely, in the conversation between Inez and Jack Lovett about the Pacific H-bomb tests in the early fifties. That conversation, we later learn, took place in 1975, after the murders. Lovett, a considerably older man, met Inez in Honolulu in 1952, before she left for college; they then had a brief affair which both remember fondly but don't resume when they occasionally meet in later years. Lovett is the antitype of Harry Victor, not a theorist and rhetorician but a sometime army officer and nominal diplomat who operates in the demimonde where the

CIA, private corporations, and plain criminals consort together for obscure purposes of national policy and personal profit. He has "access to airplanes;" when Joan Didion met him in New York in 1960 he was "running a little coup somewhere;" wherever he goes (and he goes everywhere) he strikes up conversations and asks questions, treating "information as an end in itself."

According to one idea—a cartoon idea, perhaps—of the world of power, Jack Lovett ought to be a bad man. He's certainly a tough one, whose arms deals and insurrections Didion rather gently characterizes as expressing an interesting and almost admirable "emotional solitude, a detachment that extended to questions of national or political loyalty." Compared to the ungrounded ideological sparking of loose wires like Harry Victor, Lovett's illusionless concern for how to do things, what combinations of people and materials will bring the needed result, seems in a way quite refreshing. Though Lovett isn't protected from *all* the obvious objections, Didion breathtakingly elects him to be the one who cares and remembers, the one who can transform information into knowledge, understanding, and—as his name insists—even love.

Lovett remembers those bomb tests, not as horrifying displays of abstract technique but as occasions of beauty:

> He said: the sky was this pink no painter could approximate, one of the detonation theorists used to try, a pretty fair Sunday painter, he never got it. Just never captured it, never came close. The sky was this pink and the air was wet and smelling like flowers, smelling like those flowers you used to pin in your hair when you drove out to Schofield, gardenias . . . never mind there were not too many flowers around those shot islands.

His memory of the tests overlays his memory of loving Inez at about the same time, but he does remember her. And when her life goes fully to pieces in 1975, Lovett is there to help her escape the husband and family that are destroying her.

I doubt that Didion means to suggest some comprehensive typology of character in making the otherwise sinister Jack Lovett a man of feeling in a political world where nominal good guys like Harry Victor have trouble feeling anything at all. But she does seem to have a weakness for male realists— Lovett has in effect a double in Billy Dillon, Victor's tough and cynical advisor, who understands Inez's feelings, takes care of her when her family flounders, and has secretly loved her all along. If there's a point to Lovett's combination of qualities, it may simply be that public performance doesn't reliably reveal the shape of the private self inside. Lovett's self comes to an abrupt end before *Democracy* is over, but only after he has led Inez to as much freedom as she can hope to manage; she settles in Asia, quietly looking after Vietnamese refugees, pursuing a choice of life that people like Harry Victor could never make or even understand.

*Democracy* finally earns its elaborate form. It is indeed "a hard story to tell," and the presence in it of "Joan Didion" trying to tell it right is an essential part of its subject. In a way we're all trying to learn how to tell it right, how to stop claiming what Inez finally relinquishes, "the American exemption" from having to recognize that history records not the victory of personal wills like Harry Victor's over reality but the "undertow of having and not having, the convulsions of a world largely unaffected by the individual efforts of anyone in it."

This grim message encourages the assumption that another novel called *Democracy*, by another American pessimist, Henry Adams, is somewhere in Didion's mind. (She in fact quotes from the *Education*, and Adams's ambitious, venal, magnetic, and illusionless Senator Silas P. Ratcliffe vaguely adumbrates both Harry Victor and Jack Lovett.) Both novels deal with the perilous maturing of a political culture which the national rhetoric endlessly represents as vigorous and young. Adams puts a slightly different formulation of "the American exemption" into the mouth of a European diplomat unable to stomach that rhetoric any longer:

> "You Americans believe yourselves to be exempted from the operation of general laws. You care not for experience. I have lived seventy-five years, and all that time in the midst of corruption. I am corrupt myself, only I do have the courage to proclaim it. . . . Well, I declare to you that in all my experience I have found no society which has had elements of corruption like the United States. . . . I do much regret that I have not yet one hundred years to live. If I then could come back to this city [Washington], I should find myself very much content . . . *ma parole d'honneur!*" broke out the old man with fire and gesture, "the United States will then be more corrupt than Rome under Caligula; more corrupt than the Church under Leo X; more corrupt than France under the Regent!"

Now, 104 years later, the America of Joan Didion's *Democracy*, like the America outside it, seems chillingly to confirm such a forecast. Our decline has reached the Pacific—by now a name of consummate irony—and across it. Inez Victor's businessmen relatives are making big money in construction around the Persian Gulf, but back home in the Islands their real-estate ventures are going bankrupt, and it is Wendell Omura's people who run things in Honolulu. And farther west, past the test-blast atolls, Southeast Asia testifies in its own way to the fate of imperium. Like Henry Adams, we gave up on Washington long ago.

With all due allowance for the distances between Quincy and Sacramento, Henry Adams and Joan Didion make a pretty good pair. In both of them, ironic subtlety confronts a chaotic newness that shatters older and simpler orderings. Both resist such a new reality with an essentially aristocratic weapon, the power to dispose intelligence and language, at least, against those empowered to dispose just about everything else. And both, I suppose, understand that this weapon is only defensive, and that it may not suffice.

# *After the Fall*
(1986)

*Amusing Ourselves to Death* is an all-out attack on "television culture" in the name of the print culture which Neil Postman, like some other bookish people, thinks is being destroyed by the electronic revolution. This being the case, a small moment of typographical betrayal in the book's first chapter looms larger than it otherwise would:

> I use the word "conservation" metaphorically to refer not only to speech but to all techniques and technologies that permit people of a particular culture to exchange messages.

But the message Postman brings us here is garbled—the word he has been using metaphorically is of course not "conservation" but "conversation."

In a book freer from misprints than most are in these messy times, how did this typo slip past the author and his copyeditors? Perhaps it's because both words mean such good things: as we humanly converse ("Speech . . . made us human, keeps us human, and in fact defines what human means"), we may be thinking about the shrinking wilderness, the snaildarter and the whales, dioxins and PCB's, Bhopal and Institute and Gore, Oklahoma. This "we" is an informed, concerned, *serious* segment of the whole populace, suspicious of the intentions of politicians and businessmen, anxious about the human prospect in a world that doesn't read, write, or think so good. I belong to that "we" myself, I am one of the readers Postman is looking for; but his good intentions don't lead to convincing analysis.

"Conservation" *is* in a way the word he meant. He lets us know that he deplores such as Nixon and Reagan, once worked for Ramsey Clark's senatorial campaign, and so on, but these progressive credentials are crossed by a distinctly conservative nostalgia. He yearns for a seemlier past before the Electronic Fall, our recent "descent into a vast triviality" where lurk Billy Graham, Dr. Ruth Westheimer, "Sesame Street," and talking hair-do's posing as news reporters. But it was a descent only if you make certain assumptions about the altitude of the past, and Postman's seem to me a little lofty.

Media politics, for example, is certainly a disturbing phenomenon, and Postman makes considerable sense when he looks back approvingly to a time when many people voted not for some perception of who "the best man" was (they were of course always men) but for the *party* that seemed most likely to serve their own selfish interests. But this is a complicated issue, and it isn't clarified by citing Nixon's malicious recommendation that Teddy Kennedy lose twenty pounds if he wants to be president and then observing, with curious ire, that William Howard Taft couldn't even *run* nowadays. Even if anyone wanted Taft to run, Postman has confused the issue. Had there been TV in Taft's day, his figure would have been no problem, since the taste of the time favored stoutness, male or female, presumably as evidence of solid character and economic substance. Nor am I impressed by Postman's claim that Lincoln would have done poorly in TV politics because we have no photographs of him smiling. There are precious few photographs of *anyone* smiling in the mid-nineteenth century, not because people never smiled then but because having your picture taken was understood to be a sober, formal occasion for which you dressed up and composed your features. (You didn't say "cheese" for Mathew Brady—who then would have wished to appear in even family history simpering and grinning?) In both these cases Postman adduces a complex shift of general social taste as simple proof that television has ruined our values; it was not TV alone but some intricate melding of print advertising, medical science, movies, the fashion industry, and God knows what else, that made us all want to be beaming ectomorphs.

Postman's way with example and analogy, like his governing idea of media and cultural history, derives from the late Marshall McLuhan, whom he at one point virtually equates with Plato and Locke as a Representative Thinker. Like McLuhan, Postman finds three crucial shifts in western consciousness: from orality to alphabet-writing (Fifth Century B.C.), from script to moveable type (Gutenberg), and from typography to electronic media (you know when). Like McLuhan too, he insists that each "revolution" was absolute, that these governing media are discontinuous and mutually exclusive. But there are difficulties with this. At one point Tocqueville provides him with an amusing text:

> An American cannot converse, but he can discuss, and his talk falls into a dissertation. He speaks to you as if he was addressing a meeting; and if he should chance to become warm in the discussion, he will say "Gentlemen" to the person with whom he is conversing.

There is plenty of literary evidence that American talk has had such an effect on Europeans, and "printed orality," the modeling of speech upon texts, could be expected in an isolated place like early America, remote from the easy oral fluency prevailing in European cultural centers. But Postman's theory of media history never says *how* that fluency remained available to Tocqueville and his ilk; if aural-scribal culture yielded decisively to typography in the sixteenth century, why didn't Europeans start talking like books? (McLuhan handled this one by hedging—the revolution wasn't so clearly revolutionary in Europe, where oral culture still in a way exists, but America came into being *after* the shift and has been typographical since the start.) And how is it, as Postman argues later, that only in America are the effects of TV really bad? Well, he says, it's because in other, luckier places they don't broadcast twenty-four hours a day; there are fewer channels; state control of programming precludes a really seductive variety of choice. But if, as he and McLuhan insist, not the "content" but the medium itself does the damage, not much has been explained.

McLuhan's way of playing this game always struck me as slippery, if endearingly so sometimes. Though he presented himself as a theorist and historian of perceptual technologies, he was not above a kind of hokey stagecraft that Postman likes too, as when he confides to us that Samuel F. B. Morse was "America's first true 'spaceman.'" (The quotation marks do show a twinge of shame—McLuhan wouldn't have bothered.) Or on a larger scale:

> In the late eighteenth century . . . Boston was the center of a political radicalism that ignited a shot heard round the world—a shot that could not have been fired any other place but the suburbs of Boston. At its report, all Americans, including Virginians, became Bostonians at heart.

## After the Fall

This would have come as news to Virginians like Jefferson and Madison, who for the next four decades would have more enemies in Boston than in all Europe, or to the many thousands of colonists who remained loyal to the crown. And it's surely not analysis but rhetoric that makes Postman say a paragraph later that "Today, we must look to the city of Las Vegas, Nevada, as a metaphor of our national character and aspiration." *Must* we? Might not Houston, or San Jose, or Atlanta, or even those same suburbs of Boston, now gone high-tech, afford more interesting metaphors for so large a subject?

McLuhan the information theorist always had to cope with another, more private McLuhan, the one who was a Canadian, a literary intellectual, and a convert to Catholicism, living at some spiritual and geographical remove from the electronic funhouse of post-liberal, post-Protestant America. Unlike Postman, he had moral and theological doubts about typography for its cancellation of an embracing, nurturing aural-oral ambiance that interests Postman, the resolute Gutenbergian, not at all. McLuhan tried hard to think of Global Village as a hopeful new format for the Mystical Body of Christ even as he knew that it was just the United States of America and that he ought to hate it for so crassly violating the traditional orders invoked in the great modernist writers—Joyce, Eliot, Pound, Wyndham Lewis—by whom his own cultural outlook was formed.

Postman's relation to the subject is brisker and less complex. He is an American, a liberal, a Jew; he evidently watches and even likes more television than McLuhan ever could, and few difficult private struggles seem to be going on inside him as he worries about what TV is doing to us. But his outlook is structured like McLuhan's, and I would summarize it thus:

America, he says, was until recently a literate country. It

was settled by readers—there were books on the *Mayflower*, and male literacy in colonial New England may have been as high as 95%—and it was politically fashioned by literary intellectuals like Jefferson and Hamilton. Lyceums and public libraries burgeoned in the nineteenth century; on his American tour Dickens was lionized like Mick Jagger, and *Uncle Tom's Cabin* sold 250,000 copies in its first year. Political discourse, as in the Lincoln–Douglas debates, consisted of intricate and subtle uses of language aimed at rational discrimination of ideas, and even newspapers and magazines (if only because they were printed) dealt with facts, ideas, particular forms of meaning, be they serious or trivial, true or false. But we have fallen out of this Eden into a "Peek-a-boo World" where visual images or their contentless verbal equivalents have crowded out propositional language. Various pioneers blazed the trail for television—photography, telegraphy, advertising, film (but not radio, "whose bias was . . . toward the amplification of rational speech"); but TV has completed the substituting of instantaneous, depthless, unretainable blips of information for a form of discourse whose implications could be rationally studied and judged.

Such a revolution does sound pretty bad. A nation in which, Postman says, the average child will have spent 16,000 hours watching TV by the end of high school—about 15% of waking life—is not likely to be highly literate, nor (I'd want to add) physically fit, imaginatively resourceful, or economically enterprising, which sounds equally depressing. In a sixteen-hour waking day, allowing (say) two hours for meals and snacking, seven or eight for school and travel time, one for bathing, dressing, and fixing the hair, and one or two for homework, playing records, telephoning, daydreaming, or just hanging out, two and a half hours at the tube leaves al-

*After the Fall*                                                    *187*

most no time for reading, exercise, hobbies, or part-time jobs, except on weekends. Few will read much on their own.

But *some* read, and people who grew up before television came might ask themselves if they remember many of their schoolmates doing much voluntary reading. In my own youth in the thirties and forties, bookish kids like me were oddities even in white middle-class areas like mine, and I doubt that they were more numerous elsewhere. History memorializes the heroic exceptions, the farm-children and slum-children who struggled toward fame and fortune through book-learning, and there were many more whom history never noticed. But there can never have been a general populace of readers or discerning listeners of the sort Postman has in mind, in America or anywhere else.

Postman, I think, has embraced a myth of the past that neither history nor common sense can support. He quite selectively notes fallings off between "then" and now—between, say, the sermons of Jonathan Edwards and those of Jimmy Swaggart; in the gap he puts television, and the awful truth stands revealed. (But what kind of preaching were Swift and Mark Twain so offended by?) When he claims that "the content of much of our public discourse has become dangerous nonsense," "become" just won't work. Politicians and journalists have been writing and speaking dangerous nonsense for a very long time now, and many people have believed them. My own guess is that many TV watchers are *better* equipped than their ancestors to detect the lies and evasions of public discourse by having been so inundated with what they well recognize to be the lies and evasions of television commercials.

History and common sense suffer here in other ways too. To suggest, as Postman does, that Reagan (who does just fine on radio) would be less winsome in person or even in print than he is on camera, or that Lincoln (whose enemies thought *him* a shallow buffoon) would have come across poorly on TV, is at best unprovable and at worst a hopeless scrambling of contexts. If it be assumed that *we* (just as we are now) would not vote for Lincoln, then it might follow that *they* (just as they were then) would have turned down Reagan, so that the Republic comes out about even in the never-never land of hypothesis. But in any very real world such claims make about as much sense as it would to argue that Jesus couldn't found Christianity in the television age because he looked like a hippie and because Jerry Falwell and Louis Farrakhan would see that he was Jewish.

People vote for Reagan, I suppose, not because they have lost some once universal ability to see through political rhetoric but because they think (probably rightly) that they would like and trust him as a personal friend, no matter what "politics" requires him to say, while reflecting that no one else they've voted for lately was much good at the job either. TV does of course make him more accessible to such an estimation—it has indeed changed politics, largely for the worse, but I doubt that Postman's version of history has much to do with it. For every Lincoln, there were thousands of liars, crooks, and fools elected to public office before the Fall, and some of their speeches were as good as Lincoln's. I too regret the disjunction between public language and public performance, but it might more reasonably be blamed on popular suffrage than on television.

Postman wins my heart when he confesses his distrust of "hard," quantified social science, but his own trust in anecdote and analogy doesn't inspire great confidence. Certainly his "technical" points, like so many of McLuhan's, seem quite dubious. I don't see, for example, how the format of TV news— lots of small, unconnected stories closely juxtaposed—differs technically from the format of magazines and newspapers as they evolved in the eighteenth and nineteenth centuries. It can't be some strict difference between reading and seeing-hearing, since Postman dislikes *USA Today* as much as anyone; it might be a question of the length and "depth" of treatment, since he has kind words for *The MacNeil–Lehrer News Hour*. But in effect *MacNeil–Lehrer* doesn't count, because—and here a buried motive may be emerging—so few people watch it and because MacNeil and Lehrer make so much less money than Dan Rather. To like the program, as Postman does while *not* liking a similarly "deep" but lamentably *popular* show like *60 Minutes*, doesn't compromise what may be his basic animus toward television, its highly profitable mass appeal.

But what finally makes *Amusing Ourselves to Death* an unsatisfactory treatment of its subject is not its familiar and perhaps justified resentment of how little high taste is worth in the marketplace, nor its curious hostility to visuality in general. ("Intelligence implies that one can dwell comfortably without pictures, in a field of concepts or generalizations"—it might be fun to introduce Postman to William Blake.) Rather, it's the espousal of theory at the expense of any and all experience. Postman just will not *have* a world in which some people both watch TV and read print with some awareness of what each medium is, and isn't, good for. If a photograph, simply by being non-verbal and reproducible, is a "fierce assault on language," is a recorded Beethoven quartet or a Picasso lithograph another one? a Toyota Celica? a Big Mac? But the old either/or ploy is what makes theories and theorists imposing:

> Electronic media have *decisively* and *irreversibly* changed the character of our symbolic environment. We are now a culture whose information, ideas, and

epistemology are given form by television, *not* by the printed word. To be sure, there are still readers and there are many books published, but the uses of print and reading are *not the same* as they once were [why not is never really explained]; not even in schools, the last institutions where print was thought to be *invincible*. They *delude* themselves who believe that television and print coexist, for *coexistence implies parity*. [It does? Do fleas have parity with elephants? Ghana with the Soviet Union? Jello with croquembouche?] There is *no parity* here. Print is now *merely* a *residual* epistemology, and it *will remain so*, aided to some extent by the computer, and newspapers and magazines that are made to look like television screens.

Remove or qualify the words I've italicized, and you might have something worth thinking about.

Prophets can't be pluralists, of course; for them change has to be revolution or, even better, apocalypse. But as Postman grudgingly admits, "There are many books published" (more than ever, I hear), and most of them, even the good ones, get read by somebody. If the fact that most of these readers also watch television somehow keeps them from being true readers, he should explain better what this might mean. As for all those non-readers, they were among us long before there was TV, or telegrams, or photography, or whatever it was that drove us out of the old Paradise of Letters; and we need to know just how watching television is worse for their humanity than what they used to do. For some it surely is worse, but those who once held earnest converse around the hearth or danced on the green or crafted useful articles by candlelight may have been the minority. More, I fear, worked till they dropped or drank themselves stupid or beat up their families and neighbors.

For the presumed majority about whom Postman is silent, TV may have come as a blessing, even if a more mixed blessing than it is for the lonely, the sick, and the old, its value to whom he does allow. His kind of single vision does no great harm—we can always put the qualifications and ambiguities back into the picture for ourselves. But though conservationists should worry about television, I wish that this one could sound less offended by it for not being a good public library, or by us for not always getting our reading assignments done.

# AMERICAN POPS

Next come three comments on some recent American popular novels, of various kinds and value. In writing on Robert Ludlum I wanted to ask what, if anything, thrillers tell us about who some of us are when reading certain trivial entertainments with some kind of pleasure. In discussing Stephen King, Elmore Leonard, and John Gregory Dunne I was more interested in where we are, what the scenes of contemporary life look like in such fiction. Evident here, perhaps, is my hope of finding in popular writing effects that serious criticism needn't dismiss out of hand; it may also be evident that the hope isn't easily rewarded.

# The Dark Side
(1986)

NEAR the end of *The Bourne Supremacy*, two mandarins of American covert intelligence wonder together at the feats of good field agents:

> "These people do things the rest of us only dream about, or fantasize, or watch on a screen, disbelieving every moment because it's so outrageously implausible."
>
> "We wouldn't have such dreams, or fantasies, or stay mesmerized by invention, if the fundamentals weren't in the human experience. They do what they do best just as we do what we do best."

In effect it's an apologia, or manifesto, for Robert Ludlum's outrageously implausible fiction. Though the notion that reading thrillers expresses a need to fantasize is too familiar to need thinking about, it may be useful to ask who "the rest of us" are, and what we want from such writing, as compared with what we get.

First, we are people who buy books. According to *The New York Times Book Review*, *The Bourne Supremacy* became the number one fiction best seller in its first week of publication, and many thousands of people will gladly part with twenty dollars to read it before millions more pay six or seven dollars for the paperback. We are also males—though plenty of women read mysteries and even "tough" crime fiction, I know few who would give Ludlum the time of day, or who care much for even superior espionage novels like those of John le Carré. And of course we read such thrillers when we're not out working for our money, when in fact we're lying down—in bed, in the bathtub, on the beach—or sitting in commuter trains or airplanes.

But what is it that all we recumbent, reasonably well-to-do fellows *want* from what might as well be called a ludlum? First the thing needs defining. A *ludlum*: a long, turgidly written, frantically overplotted novel, the literary equivalent of seriously wielding a plumber's helper. Its subject is conspiracy, the secret scheming of our collective enemies, foreign and domestic, and the equally secret and almost equally frightening counter-scheming of our supposed friends and protectors, the CIA or the NSC or the even more sinister "Consular Operations" branch of the State Department, which I fervently hope is Ludlum's invention. To put it more grandly, the subject is the dreadful subsumption of private selfhood and its moral sense into a morally indeterminate public life. Ludlum's heroes are respectable, successful men—lawyers, scholars, businessmen—who are entrapped and used by hidden power; some of the entrappers are on our side, some not, and the hero's task is to get them sorted out. But in an authorial move almost de rigeuer in such fiction, the difference between good and bad is kept maddeningly obscure, and the hero's fate is simply to survive and find some private happiness outside the labyrinths of power which sometimes seem to enclose us all.

*The Bourne Supremacy* is a sequel to *The Bourne Identity*, and it would baffle a reader who didn't know the earlier book (an unlikely prospect). Both novels center on David Webb, who as "Delta One" led a ruthless guerilla death-squad in Vietnam. Webb was also known and feared as "Jason Bourne," a name he took from a dead associate in this "Medusa" outfit, and in *The Bourne Identity* he is called "Cain" when his hidden masters maneuver him into collision with the terrorist "Carlos," whom he foils and almost destroys.

When *The Bourne Supremacy* begins, Webb is a partial amnesiac, living quietly in Maine with his second wife, teaching Oriental Studies at a small university and trying to erase the Delta–Bourne–Cain area of his psyche. But in Hong Kong someone calling himself Jason Bourne has begun a campaign of political assassinations that imperils the peace of just about the whole world, and Consular Operations conceives a plot to trick the real Bourne, David Webb, back into action against this imposter. Webb's wife is kidnapped, and Webb, knowing he's being recruited but not by whom, sets off to the Orient to rescue her.

I won't try to describe the layers of disinformation that Webb and the reader must peel away before the truth appears. That truth, briefly, is that a potentate in Beijing, a "philosopher-prince" named Sheng Chou Yang whom I envision as a cross between Dr. Fu Manchu and Ming the Merciless, is plotting to wreck the People's Republic and restore the Nationalists and the war lords. Sheng's chief instrument is the false Bourne, a well-born but psychotic English ex-commando, whose murders are meant to create the illusion of gang warfare among the Triads of Hong Kong. Since the Red Chinese are as terrified of organized crime as we are, they will thus be provoked into occupying Hong Kong *before* the Treaty expires in 1997, and this, Sheng cunningly foresees, will set off a general rumpus in which the Western allies and the Soviets will destroy the People's Republic, allowing him and his Taiwanese cronies to take over.

When so abruptly undressed, Ludlum's plots seem scrawny, shivering things, but in the books, as in any striptease, the audience enjoys the process more than what they finally get. Any reader of Ludlums knows that no sensible reference to geopolitical reality is intended. Nor are other sorts of realism needed, certainly not the sort that serious fiction draws on when it suggests that characters aren't wholly the servants of the writer's efficient purposes. My interest stirred, for example, when Webb, before leaving Maine to pursue his wife's abductors, paused to set back the thermostat and cancel the newspaper like any sober householder, but Ludlum was too fast for me—knowing that motive follows function, he quickly explains that Webb meant to mislead any hostile agents who might be observing him, by making it seem that he's gone away calmly and normally and can be expected back soon. The closest the book comes to suggesting irrelevant personal existence is when Webb, hiding out in a Chinese tourist hotel, hears an enraged matron from Short Hills shrieking "The toilet doesn't work and you can *forget* the phone!"

Where then does our pleasure lie? Some of it lies simply in a second-hand, low-grade tourism. The book is packed with Chinese words and Oriental scenery and food; Ludlum loves it when someone can say something like "You have good joss." We can enviously assume that he's actually been to Hong Kong, and even more enviously that he deducted the cost as "research." For us ordinary men there is vicarious pleasure too in watching a mere college professor find it in him to survive and triumph over extreme physical and moral danger. It is bracing to look out from where our reasonable, stable, somewhat boring lives are led, upon a world full of "maniacs" (Ludlum's favorite word for enemies of any persuasion), a world where each new danger is met with cries of *"Incredible!,"* *"Unbelievable!,"* *"Insane!,"* which can as easily be cries of delight as cries of dread.

Ludlum is careful to write just as badly as he can. His characters are given to remarks like "There's a rotten growth in our collective armor," and I treasure the moment when one of them, a relatively sane psychiatrist, mutters "Don't ask me where these people find their metaphors." But his conventional shoot-'em-up action prose has its own kind of interest:

# The Dark Side                                    197

The assassin threw himself over the row of flowers, clutching the warm barrel of Bourne's machine gun, wrenching it downward, leveling and firing his own gun at Jason. The bullet grazed Bourne's forehead, and in fury, Jason yanked back the trigger of the repeating weapon. Bullets thundered into the ground, the vibrations within their small, deadly arena earth-shattering. He grabbed the Englishman's gun, twisting it counter-clockwise. The assassin's mutilated right arm was no match for the man from Medusa. The gun exploded as Bourne wrenched it free. The imposter fell back on the grass, his eyes glazed, within them the knowledge that he had lost.

It would be hard for writing to make action seem less realistic than this—in such a situation, for example, who would have this preternatural awareness of what particular bullets were doing? But if the details are clumsy (did the gun "explode" or just fire?), the passage makes dim if inadvertent contact with a great tradition of violence in literature. One combatant, Webb, is called "Bourne," "Jason," and "the man from Medusa," while the other is "the assassin," "the Englishman," and "the imposter"; a firearm can be a "machine gun," a "repeating weapon," or just a "gun." If this is the elegant variation that identifies so much bad prose, still some of it sounds oddly like the variable formulaic epithets of Homeric and other oral epics, those metrical conveniences which also suggest that great men and gods and natural forces need more than one name if their magnificence is to be properly known. (The names "Jason" and "Medusa" help too.) And while I doubt that those bullets "thundered" into the ground ("thudded"?) and that very much of the earth was shattered by their "earth-shattering" impact, still the enlargement of small human violence into huge natural violence is normal and necessary in heroic writing. Neither Ludlum nor the reader needs to be conscious of such effects for them to *work* as similar ones do in the *Iliad* or *Beowulf*.

Most importantly, there is a strong if ambiguous appeal in the way Ludlum makes his heroes' motives personal ones. Those who manipulate Webb do so for the greater good even though it pains their moral sense. But when Webb is forced back into the identity of Jason Bourne, the valueless killing machine he so deeply despises, his motive is immediate and selfish: someone has taken his wife, and he wants her back. This is convenient for the author, since making Webb-Bourne the soldier of no cause but his own can offer no insult to the politics of any reader. But it also strikes a welcome note for a reader who is sick of politics altogether, worn numb by competing ideologies and slogans, wearied by endless demands that he care deeply about far-off people and places that seem no concern of his.

Webb would have refused this mission if given a choice, because he doubts his capacities and because he resents being used even for "good" purposes. But his double, "Jason Bourne," the violent, selfish, Hobbesian natural man we are born as and whom our socialized selves must bear ever after, can emerge and act with savage efficiency when Webb's civility is weakened by losing his wife. She, restored, tells him this as the book ends:

> "What do you do when there's a part of you that you hate?" said Webb.
> "Accept it," answered Marie. "We all have a dark side, David. We wish we could deny it, but we can't. It's there. Perhaps we can't exist without it. Yours is a legend called Jason Bourne, but that's all it is."
> "I loathe him."
> "He brought you back to me. That's all that matters."

Well, it's not *all* that matters, and for the reader the terms may need reversing; he may loathe not his dark side, the Old Adam within him, but the redeemed, acculturated self that goes to the office, makes deals, and tries to be liked, content to let the politicians, policemen, soldiers, and spies do the dirty work. I imagine he sometimes wonders where his dark side went, and that he welcomes any news that it may still be around somewhere or other.

# *Gulp!*
## (1986)

S<small>TEPHEN</small> King's fiction contains much that's childish, even infantile, but that alone is no scandal. We have all been children, and we carry the hidden scars of that ordeal—even a serious interest in art begins in childish make-believe. King seems to have no other subject than the ways in which childhood conceives of itself, and his resolute loyalty to that subject seems limiting and a little sad. It is, of course, also rewarding: at thirty-nine he's said to have sold fifty million copies of his twenty books. Yet his work avoids a cynical or exploitative note; I would judge that he believes in what he does, that he writes not just to make money but to exorcise demons, his own and ours.

*It* begins demonically enough in 1957, when a six-year-old has his arm torn off by what appears to be a circus clown lurking down a storm drain. This happens in Derry, Maine, where similarly dreadful events have been recorded, at intervals of about twenty-seven years, since 1741, when the entire settlement, some three hundred Yankee souls, simply vanished. The general murder rate in Derry is about six times the average for small New England cities, and Derry's young people have had a particularly rough time: in addition to many officially reported murders and "accidents," 170 kids disappeared there in 1931, and 127 in 1958, high for a town of 35,000. But even though many of the victims were later found horribly mutilated, neither the townspeople nor the press took much notice.

King organizes his grisly tale as two parallel stories, one tracing the deeds of seven unprepossessing fifth-graders ("The Losers' Club") who discovered and fought the horror in 1958, the other describing their return to Derry in 1985 when the cycle resumes. In their youth the Losers were a sorry bunch of nerds and rejects, but time (or something even more mysterious) has amply consoled them. Their leader, "Stuttering Bill" Denbrough, has become a famous horror novelist and married a movie star. Ben Hanscomb, the lonely fat kid who played with his erector set and hung out at the public library, is now trim and handsome, and also (according to *Time*) "perhaps the most promising young architect in America." Richie Tozier, the wise-cracking rock-and-roll nut who wore glasses and got good grades, is a big-time disc jockey in Los Angeles. Beverly Marsh, the tomboy from the wrong side of the tracks, is a sexy Chicago fashion designer. Eddie Kasprak, the asthmatic mama's boy who survived on vitamin pills and nasal sprays, now owns a limo company in Manhattan. Stanley Uris, the class Jew, runs his own accounting firm in Atlanta. Only Mike Hanlon stayed in Derry, to work as a librarian. Mike is black, King reveals rather late in the game, and so most of the precincts of childhood otherness are eventually heard from.

As children the Losers all had in common unpopularity, various special talents (Ben could build things, Eddie had an uncanny sense of direction, and so on), a fascination with horror movies and fantasy fiction, and a fatal allure as victims for a vicious set of schoolyard bullies. As adults they are all childless, oddly forgetful about the summer of 1958, and (except for Mike Hanlon) blessed with worldly successes which may have been arranged to distract their attention. They now remember each other only vaguely, yet when Hanlon summons them back to Derry to complete their dangerous task, they obey, except for Stan Uris, who cuts his wrists in the bath.

For readers of earlier fantasists like H. P. Lovecraft, J. R. R. Tolkien, or E. Nesbit (*It* seems a kind of ghastly take-off on Nesbit's cheerful *Five Children and It*), the story thus far is not utterly surprising. An evil something from beyond the stars has been haunting Derry since long before its European settlement, indeed since before the Ice Age. This "It" now inhabits the town's sewer system, emerging from hibernation every twenty-seven years in assorted guises—as Mr. Bob Gray, a.k.a. Pennyworth the Dancing Clown, as a syphilitic hobo who lurks in the cellar of an abandoned house and offers fellatio to passing schoolboys, or as The Creature from the Black Lagoon, Rodan, or whatever other popular monstrosity It's victims are most deeply scared by. It feeds on "the chemicals of fear," and having acquired unrecognized power over most of Derry, It aspires to a larger dominion over (gulp!) the whole world. Only brave and imaginative children, or adults who learn to remember and honor their childish selves, can hope to destroy It, as the Losers finally do in 1985.

But if the story of *It* is laughable, what sells all those books? King has not simply found and pandered to a mass audience that's too stupid to see the absurdity of his stories; I doubt that any such audience exists for books that, like his, aren't particularly easy reading. His novels are usually long and organized with some complexity, simply but not badly written, and you need to know more than comic books and B-movies to enjoy them fully. In fact it helps to have taken some courses in serious literature: the sections of *It* carry epigraphs from old rock-and-roll lyrics but also ones from W. C. Williams, George Seferis, Virgil (in Latin), Emily Dickinson, Karl Shapiro, and Dickens. And King has some fun with the educated reader when, in a flashback to the torching of a blacks-only bar by the Derry League of White Decency, he slyly names the victims after Faulknerian white folks like McCaslin, Sartoris, and Snopes.

King means to conflate cultural materials that teachers, critics, and other squares urge young people to keep separate; his is the sort of sassy muddling of high and low that *Mad* magazine was doing heavy-handedly before writers like Pynchon, Barthelme, and Coover did it so much more elegantly. King is closer to *Mad* than to Pynchon, to be sure, but he has his moments. I'm amused and touched when Mike Hanlon sees his face in the mirror as being like that of "a bank teller in a Western movie, the fellow who never has any lines, the one who just gets to put his hands up and look scared when the robbers come in." (That the teller's face was always white and Mike's is black adds a complexity that King doesn't bother to spell out.) If not exactly amused, I'm at least pleasantly startled when, at the moment when the Losers finally destroy It down in the sewers, the toilets of Derry suddenly explode, killing among others an unfortunate woman "who was sitting on the john at the time and reading the current Banana Republic catalogue." I like the remark about Hanlon's diary of the horrors by an anonymous commentator who knows King's methods: "One supposes the thought of popular publication had done more than cross Mr. Hanlon's mind." And it seems inevitable that the survivors of the Derry disaster should be interviewed on the *Today* show by Bryant Gumble and Willard Scott.

King has a nice eye for the soft spots in the commercial culture (including horror fiction itself) that is his primary connection with most of his audience, and his dislikes, which are not necessarily those of all his readers, do him credit: racism, homophobia, anti-Semitism, child abuse, machismo, social snobbery, the general staleness of feeling in Middle America. But for him such present evils are only aspects of a larger and older one, for which It is the mighty metaphor:

> It was aware of their oath, and had known they would come back. . . . When It woke It would be healed, renewed—but their childhoods would be burned away like seven fatty candles. The former power of their imaginations would be muted and weak. They would no longer imagine that there were piranha in the Ken-

duskeag or that if you stepped on a crack you might really break your mother's back or that if you killed a ladybug which lit on your shirt your house would catch fire that night. Instead, they would believe in insurance. Instead, they would believe in wine with dinner—something nice but not too pretentious, like a Pouilly-Fuissé '83, and let that breathe, waiter, would you? . . . Instead, they would believe in public television, Gary Hart, running to prevent heart attacks, giving up red meat to prevent colon cancer. They would believe in Dr. Ruth when it came to getting well fucked and Jerry Falwell when it came to getting well saved. As each year passed their dreams would grow smaller.

Both It and King are evidently neo-Wordsworthians, but readers who don't know this will still see the point. Many of them started reading him a decade or so ago, in their teens or early twenties, and millions of epigones have followed and aged a little too. No time is a good time to grow up in, but King's people have had to confront an especially nasty world, what with Vietnam, pollution, drugs, social and sexual revolutions, apartheid, mass murders and terrorism, yuppies and AIDS and the moral majority. "It" is not just a large, pregnant, spider-like monster swimming in our waste products ("They all had, after all, seen spiders before," King coolly remarks); It is a mindless wasting of human substance and possibility which we know quite enough about without reading Stephen King.

But if King's message is not news, it still is welcome, and its gothic wrappings can easily be discarded. (He seems amused himself about the requirements of his genre: "Tell your friends I am the last of a dying race," It tells a victim with a grin. "The only survivor of a dying planet. I have come to rob all the women . . . rape all the men . . . and learn to do the Peppermint Twist!") But in *It* and King's other books there's also something more uncomfortable, less a message than an unresolved anxiety. At one point Richie Dozier the disc jockey reflects about the power of the rock and roll which he purveys to make "all the skinny kids, fat kids, ugly kids, shy kids— the world's losers, in short" feel "bigger, stronger, more *there*." No doubt it does, and King, whose love of rock music and losers is open and endearing, clearly hopes that his books may have similar power. But so do uglier things like heroin and crack, or beating up smaller or weaker losers. What kind of power are we talking about, and what does it want to do? What *can* it do?

For King, the adult world is It, the devourer of imagination and of life itself. The Losers' parents are strikingly similar: Eddie's father died before the story begins, Ben's is mysteriously absent, Bill's is remote and indifferent, Beverly's is a blue-collar tyrant with incest on his mind; the other three fathers, admittedly, are fair to good, but two of them die of cancer before the story ends; the mothers, if generally more available, are smothering or ineffectual. The Losers themselves bear no children, nominally because It blocks the generation of more such enemies, but effectively, perhaps, because King needs them to remain sufficiently young at heart to destroy It once and for all—it's hard to be a child and a parent at the same time. For the book's *bad* children, the dull-witted bullies who do some of It's work and for whom family life is much harder and sadder than it is for the Losers, King strangely expresses no sympathy at all. When the worst of them actually murders his own truly monstrous father, I sense a pattern that King either isn't clearly aware of or chooses not to acknowledge. This might have private meaning—King's own father left home when his son was two, and was not heard from again; but whatever the case, the "imagination" that King would have his readers preserve from the virus of adulthood contains some grim images of hostility and aggression between the generations, between those who, like It, were here before we were and our own younger, more innocent selves.

It makes some sense to say, as King does, that art and life were Stephen King novels before he ever wrote one. Places like Derry—and all places are a little like Derry—have had their Jew-baiters and gay-bashers and child-molesters all along. It's all very well to say that the Bible is horror fiction, that Idi Amin and Jim Jones prove that monsters are real and come cheap, that one of childhood's great insights is that "Grownups are the real monsters." But having said this, what do you do next? Some part of just about everyone does grow up, learns a more complex idea of justice and obligation than children have, and suffers for having learned it. When Bill Denbrough, at age ten, sees that by persuading his comrades to believe in and resist It he is risking their lives to serve his own faith in the truth of imagination, he is appalled: "*Oh Christ*, he groaned to himself, *if this is the stuff adults have to think about I never want to grow up.*" But the joke's on him—he will grow up, all right, to think and write about this stuff just like Stephen King, and along with the philosophic mind the years will bring him a cure for his stuttering, a gorgeous and loving wife, and $800,000 a year.

*It* is King's Immortality Ode. To his young enthusiasts he keeps saying, rather loudly, Don't ever change!, even while he whispers to those who already have changed, The best is yet to be. At the end Bill Denbrough drowsily thinks: "It is good to be a child, but it is also good to be grownup and able to consider the mystery of childhood." Any adult reader can happily agree, but it's not such standard wisdom that makes *It*, or earlier and better books of King's like *Carrie, 'Salem's Lot,* and *The Shining,* so unexpectedly, if intermittently, interesting. King's sober truths are striking only when they come entangled in the popular schlock he can so deftly and fondly manipulate. If he is not a writer who asks for the most serious kind of attention, he does show us some uncharted areas of strangeness within ordinary American life.

# *The Real World*
(1987)

TOUGH crime fiction is a fairly special taste, but even those who dislike it may enjoy what Elmore Leonard makes of it, especially his way of representing common or low American voices. Consider this splendid aria from *Bandits* by an old but still frisky Louisiana bank robber banished by his relatives to a shabby nursing home:

> "My boy wanted me to stay with them, I mean live there," Cullen said. "It was Mary Jo was the problem. She'd been thinking about having a nervous breakdown ever since Joellen run off to Muscle Shoals to become a recording artist. . . . See, Mary Jo, all she knows how to do is keep house. She don't watch TV, she either waxes furniture or makes cookies or sews on buttons. I said to Tommy Junior, 'What's she do, tear 'em off so she can sew 'em back on?' I got a picture in my mind of that woman biting thread. First day I'm there, I look around, I don't see any ashtrays. There's one, but it's got buttons in it. I go to use it, Mary Jo says, 'That is not an ashtray. We don't have ashtrays in this house.' I ask her, well, how about a coffee can lid I could use? She says if I'm gonna smoke I have to do it in the backyard. Not in the front. She was afraid the neighbors might see me and then she'd have to introduce me. 'Oh, this is Tommy's dad. He's been in

the can the last twenty-seven years.' See, it's bad enough Joellen takes off with this guy says he's gonna make her a record star. Mary Jo sees *me* sleeping in her little girl's bedroom with the stuffed animals and Barbie and Ken and she can't handle it, even sewing on buttons all day. She keeps sticking her finger with the fucking needle and it's my fault. So I have to leave...."

It looks easy enough—just suppress some conjunctions and relative pronouns, start a few sentences with "See," throw in an occasional faulty verb tense or down-home locution, and life itself leaps at you off the page. But as in the "realistic" speech in Dickens or Joyce or Hemingway, not life but art creates this man, with his knack for ironic mimicy ("become a recording artist" must be how Joellen, or more likely Mary Jo, put it—Cullen himself later just says "record star"), the folkish shrewdness he discovers in a phrase like "thinking of having a nervous breakdown," his malicious fantasy of Mary Jo's regal prissiness ("We don't have ashtrays in this house") collapsing into "been in the can," a verbal betrayal by the lawless indecorum she so badly wants kept outside. Cullen sees that her obsessive sewing is comic material, and he understands, quite unforgivingly, that it comes from her powerlessness to "handle" the rest of her disappointing life.

In *Bandits* Leonard directs his art of reality toward a more difficult subject than realistic crime fiction usually takes on, the entrance of large national nightmares into domestic dreams of money and personal freedom. In New Orleans, Jack Delaney, erstwhile clothing salesman, amateur fashion model, hotel jewel thief, and convict, now works halfheartedly in his brother-in-law's funeral home. Nearing forty, educated by the Jesuits, at Tulane (for a year), and in Angola Penitentiary, Jack is no fool on his own turf, but he's not well versed in the larger world outside it; "I'm not good at environment," he cheerfully confesses, "I'm weak in those areas." But that world intrudes on his all the same, in the person of Lucy Nichols, a young ex-nun just returned from Nicaragua and its present troubles. Lucy has given up the Sisters of St. Francis but not her concern for good works, and she persuades Jack to help her save a young Nicaraguan beauty queen, Amelita Soza, whose brutal former lover, once a personal friend of Somoza and now a Contra commander, is pursuing her to kill her for (he frantically supposes) infecting him with leprosy.

Jack isn't up on the news from Central America, and his ideas of religious sisterhood lean heavily on old Joan Collins and Deborah Kerr movies and Sally Field as The Flying Nun. But Lucy is attractive enough, and his present life dull enough, to induce him to help Amelita, and also to relieve Colonel Dagoberto Godoy of the large sums he has raised from rich American right-wingers to aid the Contras. Half the loot is for Jack and the gang he recruits for the project, but he's also pleased that Lucy will take the rest to Nicaragua to help repair the harm Godoy and his sort have done.

Most of the people in *Bandits* are convincingly drawn: the tough, monstrous, but finally frivolous Godoy; his enigmatic hit man, the Miskito Indian Franklin de Dios, who loves to ask "How you doing?" but kills men as other men kill flies; Roy Hicks, the rogue cop whose nerve and ruthlessness scare even his friends; Delaney himself, whose amiable, boyish recklessness isn't big on idealistic causes but who knows that scheming and fighting for people you like is more fun than doing it just for money. The up-scale characters—Lucy and her well-connected oil-man father, who considers contributing to Godoy's secret fund but decides it's too risky an investment—are more standard. But there are lots of vivid walk-ons: the "innocent" Amelita, who casually propositions Jack when they meet; a redneck gun dealer in Gulfport who dismisses the Klan as "a bunch of negative thinkers" because they can't see that "commonism" is the real menace; Jack's old girlfriend Helene, who finds the techniques of human embalming fascinating and decides to make it her profession; even Ronald Reagan, whose testimonial letter for Godoy ("To assist you in delivering your message of freedom to all my good friends in Louisiana, I have written to each one personally to verify your credentials as a true representative of the Nicaraguan people, and to help affirm your determination to win a big one for democracy") Leonard concocts with loving care.

Godoy, however, has no intention of delivering the money to the Contras; he aims not at winning a big one for democracy but at securing a lot of big ones for himself and his drug-lord pals in Miami. This is a touch that recent news makes plausible, but it creates a difficulty in *Bandits* that Leonard's other books don't have to face. In them he deals sympathetically with people who are, or have been, criminals in at least some technical sense, or with policemen whose occupational closeness to crime makes the line between violation and enforcement rather indistinct. His is the familiar but still intriguing premise that, since no one is innocent in the old sense, everyone is potentially free to make a new self with some authentic claim to value, a value based not on learned rules but on impulsive acts that will henceforth define us. There are bad people who ignore this freedom, and they must pay the price, usually a grim one. But those who accept it may survive and prosper, though, since old rules do die hard, usually not monetarily. In the end Jack gives Lucy not half but all the Contra money, though he does still have Godoy's new sixty-thousand-dollar Mercedes to sell off, and he just may keep the proceeds.

Leonard has sometimes used geopolitical concerns as background in earlier novels—*Cat Chaser,* for one, looks back to the American intervention in the Dominican Republic in 1965. But the moral burden of public actions presses much harder than before on the personal action in *Bandits.* Godoy and his gang are not just bad *people,* Detroit street hoods or Florida dope dealers or whatever; they are agents of a sociopolitical malaise that the author, to his credit, wants us to worry about. Private guilt is not disabling in the Leonard world. Jack Delaney has stolen before and is ready, if not quite eager, to steal again, especially in a good cause. The danger isn't guilt but going back to prison, which he knows is a bad place. As a socially-conscious nun Lucy Nichols has always been on the right side, against her rich, complacent parents as well as ogres like Godoy; she has trouble thinking it wrong to steal from Godoy, even if she does it in the company of a goon like Roy Hicks, who seems as vicious as Godoy himself. But Lucy and Jack increasingly have to ask themselves if ends justify means, and even Hicks is puzzled to learn that Godoy has the sanction of certain local and federal authorities: "I want to know what side we're supposed to be on," he tells Jack, "the good guys or the bad guys." He's willing to be either, but it helps to know.

The gunman Franklin gets closer than anyone to the heart of the riddle: "Franklin de Dios was wondering if he was certain about the sides. If there were more than two sides. If he was on the side he thought he was on or on a different side. He was getting a feeling, more and more, that he was alone." (His eventual decision that he *is* alone is what makes things come out more or less justly for everyone.) And the experienced reader of Leonard may also be doing some wondering. The book has offered views of Godoy that don't mesh. Does he stand for a political nightmare in which the American government and private wealth conspire to pursue reactionary intentions, or is he just a brutal crook like those in the other novels, pursuing only the intentions of his own greed and machismo? The latter view suits the genre Leonard has perfected; to side, as we do, with Jack and Lucy is only to prefer nominal lawlessness, in otherwise good enough people, to the real and ugly thing, and that seems no problem. But the former view, in which Leonard here invests great effort and feeling, is harder, even for a reader who assumes that the real-life Contras are largely a pretext for self-corrupting conspiracies like the one the book describes. A real Godoy might of course validate both views, but Leonard's kind of art hasn't quite enough room for such complexity. *Bandits* is finally not as efficient and coherent as Leonard's best books, ones like *LaBrava, Stick,* and *Split Images;* but readers who care as much about life as about books should be glad that he tried it.

John Gregory Dunne's *The Red White and Blue* has more in common with *Bandits* than a distaste for contemporary American politics. Dunne's central character is also a youngish and rather passive Irish-American named Jack; he too comes to the difficulties of public reality through falling in love with a social activist; that reality is in both books significantly reflected by a revolution-torn country in Central America; in both, prisons and the Catholic Church are symbolic sources of energies that decisively intersect the characters' lives and fates. Leonard's deft and stylized entertainment has little else in common with Dunne's looser, darker, emotionally more taxing tale, but they do look like responses to similar worlds.

Dunne's Jack Broderick is, to his sorrow, about as privileged as an American can be. The second son of an arrogant world-class financier who gave him ten million dollars but no respect, educated at Hotchkiss and Princeton, brother of a mod Benedictine priest who once appeared on the cover of *Time* and of the sister-in-law of a glamorous young American president, compiler of a best-seller on Vietnam and now a successful Hollywood screenwriter, Jack has suffered through times that were hard for less favored people too. After college and two years in the peacetime Marines, he worked in San Francisco for one of his father's newspapers in the early 1960s, met and married Leah Kaye, a tough and notorious radical

# The Real World

lawyer, and was drawn, skeptically, into Leah's causes, most notably her successful defense of a black convict who murdered a snitch in Folsom Prison and the struggle of the Hispanic labor leader Onyx Leon to organize the California farm workers. Meanwhile Jack's brother, Dom Augustine Broderick ("Bro" to millions of media fans) finds fame in the shadowland between secular and church politics, and their sister Priscilla marries the young brother of President Frederick Griswold ("Fritz") Finn, has affairs with Fritz himself and others of his swinging circle, and dies at twenty-nine of a cerebral hemorrhage.

When his marriage to Leah fell apart in the late 1960s, Jack, always more a watcher than a doer, went to Vietnam as a correspondent, put together a book of interviews (*Grunts*) with American troops, and came home to write for the movies, marry and divorce a wealthy nymphomaniac, and observe the weird displacements of radical energies as old causes dwindled down. In the early 1980s he encounters Leah again, in the Central American country of Cristo Rey, where she is helping a human-rights organization monitor the behavior of a repressive junta beset by revolution. Things go very badly in Cristo Rey. An American nun in Leah's group is raped and killed by a government death squad; Onyx Leon is found murdered, his severed head stuffed into the stomach of a dead peasant woman; the bombing of a government-sponsored beauty pageant ("Miss Global Village"), around which Jack is trying to construct a silly movie, sets off a gun battle which kills Miss Thailand and an effeminate piano-player. Back in San Francisco, history deals Jack his worst blow yet, when Bro and Leah, despite their failings the only people he has ever loved, are gunned down on the steps of Glide Memorial by Richie Kane, an embittered Vietnam vet whom Jack had interviewed in *Grunts* and now a failed candidate for county supervisor on an anti-gay ticket. Jack understandably decides to leave America, perhaps permanently.

*The Red White and Blue* is designed like a movie, with lots of flashbacks and cross-cutting, and Dunne, a sometime screenwriter himself, makes the method work; the book is powerful, often both funny and horrifying, and seldom dull. Since my reservations about it may sound like futile protests against modern life itself, I should say right away that, scene by scene, nothing Dunne shows us exceeds modern life's power to appall. Yet I sense cumulative distortion in which overdetermined artistic choices—a determination to make things *really* bad—interfere with the representation of a public reality that is already quite bad enough.

In the book moral horror takes the form of visceral disgust which is achieved only through a certain amount of authorial rigging. For example, the criminal whose acquittal wins Leah Kaye her fame as an advocate is (rightly) charged with having directed the prison murder of a stool-pigeon; the victim drowned when seventeen other convicts urinated in his mouth while he was tied down. That seems pretty bad, but then life can be pretty bad, in Folsom or outside it. But for Jack the horror centers on his learning that the drownee's mouth was propped open with the stub of "a number three soft Dixon Ticonderoga" pencil. Jack feels that he ought not to have to know this "appalling simplicity," that the detail makes too vivid an event that should only more vaguely imaginable. The question seems to be, How tough are you?, and Jack evidently isn't tough enough. His way out is to deplore the "passion for specificity" of the TV news reporter (then his mistress) who calmly tells him about the pencil, and we may suppose either that Dunne also sees the detaching of such data from their human implications as a major sign of what's gone wrong with us or that he's challenging us to be as tough about life as he is. But of course there's no "life" here—no pencil, no reporter, no Jack, no such murder—except in the words Dunne himself elected to write the episode with. To be a little simple-minded about it, whatever comparable horrors life may be able to supply, *this* horror exists in the writing of someone who yet proposes it as proof of how dreadful recent reality has been.

All art, to be sure, invents its evidences of the real. The question is how it is done, in what moods, with what intentions of effect, and here I think *The Red White and Blue* is vulnerable. Dunne is too fond of planting effects that can then be both scorned and exploited. Early in the book, for example, Jack is amused and offended by a vulgar movie producer's formula for good box-office: "Nuns and midgets, that's the ticket. Your story's got a nun or midget in it, you can't go wrong." Yet almost immediately Jack confesses to us that *his* story, this book, will contain both a nun and a midget, as Dunne of course has determined that it will. Or later, after reporting some scabrous remarks by his terrible father about Fulton J. Sheen, Clare and Henry Luce, and Dwight Eisenhower, Jack remarks that "As always I was amazed by my father's capacity for slander," as if it weren't Jack's own readiness to repeat such entertaining slurs, and behind that the author's pleasure in making them up in the first place, that effectively created the moment.

Nor am I as appalled as Dunne evidently wants me to be as I follow the book's relentless measurement of people and their acts against the direst ideas available of what is human, as if the admitted reality of crotches and underwear, vaginal yeasts and crabs, casual fornication and fellatio and toilet paper, somehow said about all that needs saying about the species. Vomiting and diarrhea here seem as routine as eating and breathing; it becomes almost predictable that a priest should wear a colostomy bag, that Jack should propose to Leah while sitting on a bidet, that a prisoner should be gassed in San Quentin while bleeding to death after trying to slash his throat, that a soldier should be blown up while masturbating in a latrine, that the suicide of another soldier should accidentally reveal, and kill, two of his buddies in homosexual congress in the next room. The problem is not taste or credibility, but a sense that the writing has locked itself into a cruelly narrow range of figurative resources, which it is doomed to repeat endlessly in ever more Baroque extravagance. When Dunne gives us a nightclub bouncer who's asphyxiated during after-hours coitus on a grand piano rigged to descend on wires when a grand entrance is required—the poor man is crushed against the ceiling when the contraption accidentally goes back up, though his stripper partner survives because her silicone breast-implants give her some breathing room—one scarcely can know what to feel.

Somewhere in the midst of such stuff the serious horror of living in times like this gives way to the fun of inventing newer and wilder horrors. Like Swift and Céline, Dunne sometimes seems over-ready to despair of us for being made of flesh and blood, with organs and wastes inside, too interested in the old body-sex-death nexus to let mere social and political disgust seem the main objective. There are fine things in this novel; Dunne's ear for American speech is at least in Elmore Leonard's league, and he gives us keenly-observed versions of a grotesque Hollywood funeral service, geriatric man-talk at the Bohemian Grove, the soft cant of show-biz radicals and the hard cant of big-time pols and the nowhere cant of graceless losers and haters like Richie Kane. But there may be too much material here for one fully coherent novel, and too much determination never to get caught in the company of some cheap little illusion or other.

At one point Jack Broderick tries to mourn for the murdered nun whom Bro's facile liberal eloquence inspired to try to improve what she called "the real world":

# The Real World

The real world. She had no idea that the real world inhabited by Bro was the world of Mingo Coolidge [a reactionary Senator] and Dominick LoBianco [a Philadelphia mafioso] and eighty-pound cardinals who knew the numbers of all the secret bank accounts and a sister who committed adultery with the President of the United States, who considered cocoon a synonym for n-nigger. Phyllis Emmett was spectacularly unequipped for this world, which was perhaps why she ended up in the red clay of Chalatenango Province, Cristo Rey, C. A., her Lily of France cotton bikini bottoms inside out and backside front around her ankles.

I doubt that very many people are well equipped for a world like that; but when you can't bear not to see through everything, what you see behind it all does look pretty much the same. As one who hopes that the terms of our present life are not *equally* dreadful, that some evils mean more than others, I suspect that Dunne's indictment of American experience in our time is too extravagant and sweeping to seem unanswerable.

*That Tom Wolfe should figure so much in this chronicle is perhaps inevitable—he does have a way of finding topics of the times and giving them provocative, or at least provoking, expression. Here it's the insubstantial affluence of the Roaring Eighties and the social and racial tensions it has generated. That Wolfe would turn this worthy subject into a psychodrama of the gratifying, even heroic resistance of privilege to the low aspirations of the inelegant masses was no doubt to be expected. But the villain of the piece is not Wolfe himself but the many readers who took* The Bonfire of the Vanities *to be a serious social commentary, when they really should have known better.*

## *Small Expectations*
(1988)

AUTHORS are not responsible for what even their friendliest critics say about them, and I can't blame Tom Wolfe for George Will's statement that *The Bonfire of the Vanities*, Wolfe's first novel, is "Victorian, even Dickensian" in its scope and its "capacity to convey and provoke indignation." Both Dickens and Wolfe, to be sure, are broad, even outrageous social comedians, always ready to convert observation into drama, or melodrama, in which conflicting human desires suggest pathological disturbances within the body politic. But Dickens also had the artist's saving interest in mystery. He knew how to hold his readers by concealing the connections between characters and events just as long as possible, and he knew that in serious fiction even caricatures should be hard to see all the way around, that they can suggest more than their assigned roles require.

Tom Wolfe has no discernible interest in mystery. Since his characters must mean what he wants them to mean, they can exist only externally—in their clothes, their accents, their living arrangements or colleges or cars, their places of work or play—and the fun for the author is to read us their IDs and spot them right away for what they are. They are, by and large, people who say "tawk" for "talk," or wear "half-brogued New & Lingwood shoes with the close soles and the beveled insteps," or cultivate overdeveloped sternocleidomastoid muscles.

Wolfe feels free to mock characters whose souls are subsumed in such surfaces, yet without their surfaces he would be at a loss to know who they are. When in *Great Expectations* the newly gentrified Pip entertains Joe Gargery in London, the awkwardness of the occasion is conveyed by the way Joe's hat insists on falling off the mantlepiece, but while we can be sure that Joe has worn the wrong kind of hat, the meaning is not *in* the hat or its style but in how both men use it—Joe by endlessly fumbling with it, Pip by watching it so impatiently—as a way of withholding some vulnerable part of themselves from a reunion that embarrasses them both, at the time, and deeply shames the wiser Pip who describes the event long after it has taken place. There is nothing like this in Wolfe's repertory.

*The Bonfire of the Vanities* is the story of Sherman McCoy (Buckley, St. Paul's, Yale), who at thirty-eight is *"going broke on a million dollars a year!"* McCoy is the star bond trader for a leading New York investment banking firm (probably he'd be making more than a million, but never mind), yet his strange incompetence at personal finance has put him deeply in the red. One can understand the house in Southampton, the four servants, the private school tuitions, the cars and clothes and dinner parties, but not why someone not limitlessly rich, who knows about debt, would buy a co-op in a building that forbids mortgages, so that he has to take out a short-term personal loan, interest non-deductable, for almost two million dollars. Still there are at least a few dumbbells on Wall Street, and one can feel a little sorry for fatuous weaklings like McCoy who fancy themselves "Masters of the Universe."

Wolfe's governing subject, the decline of the old-line WASPs in crude times, requires that McCoy be sprung from old money, born to expect privilege without having to work or fight for it. His father in fact is the retired "chief executive officer"—for which read "senior partner"?—of the major cor-

## Small Expectations

porate law firm of Dunning Sponget & Leach. Yet Sherman doesn't think like someone familiar with wealth and power:

> Just think of the millions, from all over the globe, who yearned to be on the island, in those towers, in those narrow streets! There it was, the Rome, the Paris, the London of the twentieth century, the city of ambition, the dense magnetic rock, the irresistible destination of all those who insist on being *where things are happening*—and he was among the victors! He lived on Park Avenue, the street of dreams! He worked on Wall Street, fifty floors up, for the legendary Pierce & Pierce, overlooking the world! He was at the wheel of a $48,000 roadster with one of the most beautiful women in New York—no Comp. Lit. scholar, perhaps, but gorgeous—beside him! A frisky young animal! He was of that breed whose natural destiny it was . . . to have what they wanted!

The mind being burlesqued here can't be Sherman McCoy's; no one of his background would think in the rapt clichés of the overwrought newcomer, any more than he would have Sherman's self-consciousness about the "statement" his clothes make. Even Jay Gatsby would blush at having to say such lines.

At any rate, Sherman, deep in such out-of-town ecstacies, misses the Manhattan turn-off from the Triborough Bridge and gets himself and his frisky mistress, Maria Ruskin, thoroughly lost in the South Bronx. Encountering two black youths whose intentions seem dubious, they flee, with Maria at the wheel, while sensing that the car may have struck one of the kids. Fearing discovery of their affair by their spouses, they decide not to report what they're not sure was an injury. But in fact they have hurt a respectable teenager, and from that event issues Sherman's nightmare introduction to the world other people inhabit. Under pressure from the Reverend Reginald Bacon, a politically potent black activist who feeds privately at the troughs of public and private assistance programs, the police trace the car to McCoy. The prospect of a "great white defendant" is of course grist for many mills besides Bacon's: the Bronx DA is facing reelection in a hugely nonwhite, nonrich borough; one of his assistants is anxious to impress his new girlfriend with his courtroom prowess; the victim's companion is only too ready to perjure himself to beat a drug rap; a seedy British journalist at a sensational tabloid, *The City Light,* needs a hot story to save his job; even Maria, after first fleeing to Italy, agrees to testify that McCoy, not she, was driving. Sherman is arrested and booked, indicted, reviled in the media and in various mass demonstrations, and finally brought to trial for reckless endangerment and leaving the scene of an accident, losing along the way his wife, his job, the big deal that was to pay off his debts, and worst of all, his illusions of mastery.

This story allows Wolfe, in propria persona or through the mind of Sherman McCoy, to say a lot of unpleasant things about most of the residents of New York—WASPs, blacks, Hispanics, Jews (especially rich ones and Hassidim), gays and lesbians, liberals, Brits, social activists, urban (but not national) politicians, social climbers, journalists, smokers and drinkers, food and clothes snobs, the fat and the thin, exercisers, people with New York accents, and so on. He tends to like policemen, criminal lawyers (especially ones who are sharp dressers and went to Yale Law School), Art Deco, and judges, but the world pictured is mainly a theater of malice, and it seems tempting to ask why the book has sold so well. No doubt many of the customers are metropolitan people ready to laugh at the pretentious follies of, if not exactly themselves,

## Small Expectations

then people like the ones they know. But elsewhere in the Republic some may be reading *The Bonfire of the Vanities* more innocently, as the morality play its title suggests it to be. Do such readers, not knowing people like the ones Wolfe describes (and glad of it), imagine that the book, like certain magazines and TV shows, gives believable glimpses of the rich and famous, along with some of the poor and dangerous who are equally stimulating to the powers of moral censure?

Sherman McCoy's career follows an interesting curve. He begins as a weak, cosseted fool, a man without talent or conviction blessed (like so many others) by living in a time when one can do quite nicely without having either. He's not guilty, or not very guilty, of much but hubris, yet a society in which the worst have usurped the power Sherman's class once held makes sure that he will pay dearly for being white and privileged. His shame and fear in the luridly described holding pens at Bronx Criminal Court seem at first to him a kind of death, but what really is dying is his assumption that he can live as he wants to without effort.

As the story nears its end he starts to fight back, telling off those of his own circle who have ignored or exploited his disaster, betraying the mistress who has already betrayed him, and finally, in an exciting but preposterous climax, when a rabid courtroom of blacks and do-gooders attack both him and the courageous judge who has dismissed the charges against him, claiming his manhood through redemptive physical violence:

> That sets the mob off. *Yagggghhh!* . . . *Ged'im!* . . . *Ged'im!* . . . Shoving past the court officers. Brucie pushes the tall black man with the earring. He goes reeling to one side. All at once he's directly in front of Sherman. He stares. He's amazed. Face to face! And now what? He ducks, pivots on his hip, and turns his

back—*now!*—*it begins now!* He wheels and drives his fist into the man's solar plexus.
    "Ooooo!" . . .
    "Sherm!" It's Quigley, talking between gasps. "You cold-cocked . . . that cocksucker! . . . Sherm! You . . . cold-cocked him!"
    *Sank to the floor. Doubled up. The earring dangled. Now!*—*and I triumphed.* He's consumed with cold fear—*they'll get me!*—and soaring anticipation. *Again! I want to do it again!*

    Whatever this ugly moment means—the true machismo of the paramilitary racist groups? the hopeless dream of glory that all little people dream but very seldom try to enact?—it seems clear that for once Wolfe has rendered a character's mind very well. He knows that the main thing isn't striking the blow but relishing it afterward, wanting to do it again. Whatever the author intends, I'd be surprised if there weren't readers out there for whom the moment represents a welcome stirring of counterrevolution, wiping out the space in which law, sympathy, generosity, and patience stand between a resentful "us" and a "them" who have taken what we once had and still want. Another Sherman McCoy emerges here, the real McCoy, perhaps, a feral fellow who won't be pushed around anymore, as is confirmed at the end of the book, when McCoy appears for his second arraignment, for manslaughter, wearing not a two thousand dollar suit but "an open-necked sport shirt, Khaki pants, and hiking shoes." The outfit sounds like a call to arms for anyone who wants to hear one.
    Power has always been Wolfe's subject. When, in his earlier journalism, it took the form of populist cultural power subverting established taste from below—in the rock music industry, car customizers, surfers, or druggies—he could write from his strongest position, laughing at his readers for

fearing "vulgar" vitality even while he knew that it *was* vulgar, and ludicrous too. When the material is more overtly political, however, as in *Radical Chic* and now *The Bonfire of the Vanities,* the case is somewhat altered and the laughter grows nastier. Here is his portrait of a charmless Jewish assistant DA musing on the consolations of his office:

> In that instant . . . his scuffed attaché case meant nothing, nor did his clodhopper shoes nor his cheap suit nor his measly salary nor his New York accent nor his barbarisms and solecisms of speech. For in that moment he had something that these Wasp counselors, these immaculate Wall Street partners . . . would never know and never feel the inexpressible pleasure of possessing. And they would . . . swallow with fear when and if their time came. . . . It was the power of the government over the freedom of its subjects. To think of it in the abstract made it seem so theoretical and academic, but to *feel* it . . . well, the poet has never sung of that ecstacy or even dreamed of it, and no prosecutor, no judge, no cop, no income-tax auditor will ever enlighten him, for we dare not even mention it to one another, do we?—and yet we *feel* it and we *know* it every time they look at us with those eyes that beg for mercy or, if not mercy, Lord, dumb luck or capricious generosity. (Just one break!)

Wolfe enjoys scaring the libertarian in us with the spectacle of government licking its chops, but I suppose that any form of power feels something like this when it's consciously exercised (as fortunately it more often is not), as employers, teachers, pastors, plumbers, parents, athletes, and rioters probably could testify. And even if civil servants relish their power more, I doubt that it's the differences in costume and speech habits between them and their victims that set off their ecstasies. (Wolfe in fact has to cheat a little here—those "clodhopper shoes" appear to be the same ones this man wore earlier in the book, when they were described as Johnston & Murphy business shoes he was afraid to wear on the subway, where their evident costliness might attract muggers.) The passage expresses not authentic malice in a disgruntled public employee but a projection onto him of the anxieties "superior" people may feel about how someone potentially hostile and dangerous perceives them.

Wolfe manages to have class hostility both ways. The old WASP establishment, he says, is now dispossessed without quite knowing it; New York and places like it have fallen to the sansculottes, ethnic whites and (now) nonwhites who have learned how to manipulate and profit from the system just as their predecessors did. It's a good joke on any WASP who didn't already know this, but the "indignation" George Will praises Wolfe for provoking may be less healthily self-critical than Will wants to suppose. He reads the novel as saying that "flocking to Wall Street . . . is . . . unworthy of 'the sons of the great universities, those legatees of Jefferson, Emerson, Thoreau, William James, . . . inheritors of the lux and the veritas.' " Wolfe does say this—though there are fewer of Sherman McCoy's crowd in present-day Wall Street trading rooms than he suggests—but the book is in touch with other, far less pious kinds of indignation too.

Yet this probably isn't the "conservative novel" Will has been hoping for, or indeed a political novel at all. The depth and acuity of Wolfe's idea of politics are suggested by his quoting the old joke that "a liberal is a conservative who has been arrested," which of course reads at least as well the other way round. His main interest seems better represented by something McCoy tells his young daughter when he tries to prepare

# Small Expectations 229

her for hearing that he has been arrested: "There are bad people who want to believe bad things about other people." Tom Wolfe thrives on saying bad things about other people to people he suspects are pretty bad themselves. This game is entertaining enough; as a novelist Wolfe is at least somewhat wittier than Sidney Sheldon and less sentimental than Jimmy Breslin. But *The Bonfire of the Vanities* is not worth taking seriously, and it has nothing to do with Dickens.

A Fan's Notes *appeared in 1968, the year this chronicle began, and Frederick Exley provides it a kind of retrospective, elegiac way of ending. His is largely a record of failure, as a writer and (by his own account, at least) as a man. But the failure of his dreams of stardom points not just to his own special deficiencies but to much of what "success" had generally come to mean in America in our time, and there is something admirable, and very American, about someone who, like Melville's Bartleby, in effect* chooses *to fail in a world whose official values seem to him hopelessly unacceptable.*

# Macho Man
(1989)

THE appearance of *Last Notes from Home* encourages an assessment of a curious literary career. Frederick Exley's is not a large or copious talent; he's published three books in twenty-one years, and only one of them could be called a clear, if odd, success. But in various ways all three tell some of the truth about the imagination in a culture like ours, and even their faults seem instructive and touching.

In *Last Notes from Home* the author insists that "I have never written a single sentence about Frederick Exley except as he exists as a created character," which seems a repeat of what he said in introducing *A Fan's Notes* (1968): "I ask to be judged as a writer of fantasy." Evidently he knows what happens when experience is expressed in language, the impossibility of self-revelation that isn't also self-invention. But in his case the space between author and work seems unusually narrow. *Pages from a Cold Island* (1975) in fact called itself "nonfiction," and anyone interested in Frederick Exley's writings about the life and troubles of "Frederick Exley" probably hopes that they're in some sense true, that the two Exleys are close relatives, connected at least by the mutual irritation that, quite as strongly as affection, attaches us to our own families.

Yet decency calls for a distinction between the writer of these books, whom I shall call "Exley," and his protagonist and narrator, who can be given the nickname he and others use, "Ex." (An alert explorer of self-ironies, Exley surprisingly never comments on this one: "Ex" as "former, lost, failed," or, as pronounced, "X," the nameless man, the unknown quantity.) Ex is a mess—an alcoholic, a sometime mental patient, a man who couldn't keep a job or a wife, a sponger off his friends, a rolling stone incurably nostalgic for his roots, a talented athlete gone to pot and reduced to fandom. The bars of every American town have their Exes, most of whom doubtless feel in their own terms the desire that Exley uses Hawthorne's terms for (in *Fanshawe*) as an epigraph to *A Fan's Notes:* "If his inmost heart could have been laid open, there would have been discovered that dream of undying fame; which, dream as it is, is more powerful than a thousand realities."

Fame is the spur, certainly, for *A Fan's Notes,* a strangely powerful book which won attention and praise in the late 1960s but whose poor sales made Ex sure it was a failure. It begins around 1962 in Ex's (and Exley's) home town, Watertown, New York, where Ex, in his early thirties and full of anxiety, defiance, and self-loathing, is teaching English in a local high school, drinking heavily on weekends, and undergoing a divorce. Gradually a personal history is assembled. Ex is the son of a memorably gifted local sports hero who passed up college and big-time stardom to get married, raise a family on his earnings as a lineman for Niagara Mohawk, and die at forty of lung cancer. Ex himself was a good if undersized high-school football and basketball player; he made it to college, with difficulty and not as an athlete, graduated from USC in 1953, and went on to various jobs, sexual adventures, and a marriage to an upper-class girl from Westchester.

In the midst of this not unusual early career, he collapsed. He gave up any pretence of working, went home to his mother's house to lie for months on the couch, eating Oreo cookies and watching TV soaps, and eventually had to be institutionalized, not for the last time, as a paranoiac. It was in the asylum that he began writing, and after his release he kept working on a novel that sounds something like *The Man in the Gray Flannel Suit,* one more tragedy of the spirit defeated by the organized conformity. At the time of the telling, he has accomplished nothing, and his imagination devotes its powers to televised sports, the window on a freedom of possibility that American life kept withholding from people like him.

At USC Ex had been a contemporary of the great Frank Gifford, and though he never saw him play football in college and indeed only laid eyes on him once or twice, watching Gifford and the Giants, on Sunday afternoons in Watertown bars, became vital to Ex in his ruin. "Why did football bring me so to life?" is the book's most interesting question, considerably more interesting than most of Ex's answers, that it was "direct" or "traditional" or whatever. It of course wasn't football itself that led him to "life" but his yearning identification with the image of Gifford on the screen, with the way his skills made real the player's own fantasies, turning intention into fact as Ex's writings couldn't do. But there was more to it than that:

> I cheered for him with such inordinate enthusiasm, my yearning became so involved with his desire to escape life's bleak anonymity, that after a time he became my alter ego, that part of me which had its being in the competitive world of men; I came, as incredible as it seems to me now, to believe that I was, in some magical way, an actual instrument of his success. Each time I heard the roar of the crowd, it roared in my ears as much for me as him; that roar was not only a promise of my fame, it was its unequivocal assurance.

As Ex understands, such extreme obsession lies near to madness. But tuned down a little, it's what drives any fan or groupie or celebrity junkie, out here where fame is harder to come by more directly, and those utterly immune to such "magic" could hardly be said to be alive at all.

Still, Ex's version of such obsession *is* extreme; the night after he saw (live, for once) Gifford get blind-sided and nearly killed by Chuck Bednarik of the Eagles, he picked a drunken fight with two strangers in Greenwich Village and nearly got killed himself. It's the extremity, not the stilted writing ("alter ego" indeed!) or the familiar idea about identification, that makes the perception so disturbing. Even good writing about sports seldom confesses that fans are, however briefly and benignly, crazy, that they're not just fanciers or fantasists but fanatics, caught up in a desire that is literally self-destructive, a desire not to be what they are—anonymous, mortal—but to be as one with fame as the religious hope to be with God. (The famous themselves are of small consequence—Frank Gifford, though he's been on TV on fall Monday nights for two decades and is far more famous, or at least famous to more people, than he ever was as a player, is never even mentioned in Exley's later books; Ex simply found other people to be magical for him.) The extremity is what makes the book so expressive of what the 1960s, with their passionate, narcissistic attachments to figures and causes outside the self, were like even for the relatively sane.

Obsession of this sort is what gives a center to the larger concern of *A Fan's Notes*, the vulnerability of any life to madness, and also its possible remedy, the conversion of life into imaginative acts, themselves forms of (roughly speaking) madness but ones within which a better kind of being may be intimated. Ex the jock is really an aesthete, musing on Frank Gifford as Keats mused on Grecian urns and nightingales. He doesn't write like Keats, but even an awkward style can be expressive of something:

It occurs to me now that my enthusiasms might better have been placed with God or Literature or Humanity [than with football]; but in the penumbra of such upper-case pieties I have always experienced an excessive timidity rendering me tongue-tied or forcing me to emit the brutal cynicisms with which the illiterate confront things they do not understand.

Such verbal fumbling can at least suggest that something is fighting its way through language's disposition toward suave distortion and lying. To say it (whatever "it" is) too well and eloquently might destroy it, and if like Ex you're defiantly proud of what's wrong with you, the cure of effective expression may be shamingly worse than the disease.

For both Ex and Exley, health and disease, strength and weakness, are parts of the same idea. Athleticism and its decline in drunkenness and paranoia, romance and sexual adventurism, performance and impotence, pride in family and place and the need to escape them, personal honor and a fascination with criminality—all such polarities help to portray Ex as what he calls himself and wants to be, "a self-destructively romantic man." But they also say something about America in his time.

In the asylum Ex discovered that confirmed lunatics are *ugly*. "They had crossed eyes and bug eyes and cavernous eyes. They had club feet or twisted limbs or—sometimes—no limbs." A nation "drunk on physical comeliness" could have no place for such as them, or, if he could make himself and his life ugly enough, for him either. He found the gloss of modern American surfaces, the living-room chic purveyed by TV and advertising, embodied in the person of Bunny Sue Allorgee ("allergy"? "allegory"?), the ravishing all-American beauty from Chicago who offers herself to an avid Ex but with whom he just can't make it. Later he decides that "my inability to couple had not been with her but with some aspect of America with which I could not have lived successfully," a repudiation which his abortive career as an aluminum siding salesman expresses perhaps more wittily.

In the madhouse he learned that accepting one's madness, preferring ugliness to its meretricious alternative, "may be the only redemption in America," and *A Fan's Notes* ends with an appropriate nightmare of aesthetic confrontation, in which Ex, mistaken for a Peace Walker from his scruffy appearance, gets beaten up by a convertibleful of Dan Quayle prototypes, interchangeably handsome college-boy hawks in cashmere sweaters and Bermuda shorts, "the generation to whom President Johnson has promised his Great Society," "this new, this incomprehensible America" whose middle class will never have to know poverty, defeat, disease, remorse, or ugliness, and hence never need creative passion.

This was a shrewd perception in 1968, but Exley's second book, *Pages from a Cold Island,* couldn't find a lot to say about the new America. It's a portrait of the artist at loose ends, unable to pursue the fame that *A Fan's Notes* brought teasingly near but did not quite confer. Ex is now a minor man of letters who's won awards, gotten to know some of his literary confreres, been invited to teach at the Iowa Writer's Workshop, and so on. He can't finish his new book, called *Pages from a Cold Island* but evidently not the book we are reading. He lives mostly on a warm island, in Florida, drinking steadily in the bar next to his hotel, while outside golden teen-agers are boozing and getting high and, farther away, the McGovern campaign is sinking fast. But public events are not Ex's concern; what continuity the book has comes from his obsessive pursuit of Edmund Wilson—not the man, who has recently died and whom Ex could never contrive to meet anyway, but the career, the fame, the aura of greatness Ex still hasn't achieved for himself.

The odd-sounding substitution of Wilson for Gifford derives from Ex's keen sense of the mana of locale. In the *Last Notes from Home* he takes a horrified pride in knowing that the Dulles brothers were Watertown boys too, and in *A Fan's Notes* he was astonished and pleased to learn that Wilson's upstate town of Talcottville was only a few miles south of Watertown. Now he pursues various survivors of "the legendary critic"— Wilson's wife and daughter, local friends—seeking verbal and physical relics of such sanctity. (At one point he asks for, and is refused, one of Wilson's walking sticks.) Exley had been writing an article on Wilson for the *Atlantic,* and it seems too clear that *Pages from a Cold Island* is largely a conflation of that piece with another, for *Playboy,* on Gloria Steinem. Wilson provides Ex an occasion to speculate on literary fame, and Steinem, who, he notes, became a celebrity despite humble origins not unlike his, allows him to examine his own nervousness about feminism, the New Politics, and his rather alarming tendencies toward misogynism.

But Ex's reports on Wilson, Steinem, and the other greats and semigreats he's met, seen, or lived near don't advance the points made earlier, with less effort, through Gifford the football star. And otherwise the book is a farrago of personal odds and ends—not very original critical views of Nabokov, Mailer, Kate Millet, and others, a disapproving comparison of Ben Gazzara with Brando, favorite recipes and meals done in menu prose ("great bowls of salad with chunks of tomato, fresh mushrooms, anchovy, Bermuda onion, and Italian dressing garnished sumptuously with Parmesan cheese"), and touring guides ("From Snow Ridge one motors to Houseville and up into Martinsburg . . . and at the latter one begins a miles-long descent into the idyllic, shaded, brick and clapboarded village of Lowville, the county seat of Lewis County, where one again picks up the main Route 12 north"). One looks in vain for signs that Ex is kidding us, or himself; the book is a kind of vacuum sucking in whatever language may be somewhere around, or anecdotes about people Ex met in bars or airports, about the wondrous girls he met and made, about the cozy comraderie of watering holes like his local in Florida.

It's a sad, baffled book, hard not to take as evidence of a talent in dissolution from rather ordinary causes. Near the end of it Ex quotes from a letter written to him by his older brother, a career soldier, who rebukes Ex's confession of being deeply afraid of life by saying, "I do not accept your fears." Whatever their status may be elsewhere, in this book they don't seem acceptable, and the reader may be tempted to endorse what Ex amusedly calls Colonel Exley's "military solution": "Get off the sauce!"

He isn't yet off it in *Last Notes from Home,* which is full of hard drinking, remembered sex, and general irresponsibility. Whatever may have happened to Ex since the 1970s isn't in the book, which he says he's writing in 1978 and which begins in 1973, before *Pages from a Cold Island* was finished. But *Last Notes from Home,* though full as ever of digressions, has a story of sorts to tell.

Ex visits Hawaii in 1973 to be with his brother, the colonel, who is dying of cancer. On the long flight over he falls in with two familiar but vivid types, his seatmate Jimmy O'Twoomey, an aging drunk and professional Irishman from Dublin, and Robin Glenn, a gorgeous and very obliging flight attendant. Robin, it emerges, has a profitable sideline as a high-priced Honolulu hooker and mistress to a rich businessman; O'Twoomey, supposedly a PR man for the Irish Hospital Sweepstakes, seems on closer acquaintance to be a high official of the IRA Provos and also, he says, an Irish peer, though barred, as a citizen of Eire, from assuming his seat in the Lords. As Ex suffers through the death of "the Brigadier," as he's called his brother since childhood, he gets ever more involved with Robin, who determines to marry him, and with O'Twoomey, who's not too busy with his secret arms deals to set Robin up in the travel business and hold Ex in princely captivity on Lanai, hoping to get him dried out and force him to marry Robin and finish *Pages from a Cold Island*.

Into this comic thriller Ex as usual unloads whatever happens to be on his mind. A travelogue on Punchbowl Cemetery; critiques of *Gunsmoke, Hawaii 5-0,* Edna Ferber, Joyce, and others; disquisitions on the Korean War, the internment of the Nisei, the My Lai massacre, Watergate, high-school football coaching, the killing of Martin Luther King, Jr., the Women's Movement—no subject catches him without an opinion, however commonplace. But the story is full of surprises. O'Twoomey, it turns out, is not in the IRA at all—he's just a "filthy rich looney" who's read too many spy novels and wants badly to be a character in Ex's book. The Brigadier died not from cancer but from the physical and moral attrition of his terrible work for Military Intelligence in Vietnam, where he may even have done the targeting for the My Lai operation. And Robin is another of the female fantasists and hysterics who have dogged Ex all his life; her stories about her well-to-do background and unceasing sexual abuse—by her father, by the janitor of her boarding-school dorm, by an insatiable Ivy League quarterback—are all just lies. But while Ex recognizes her as yet another "brute American male fantasy of the cornbread princess," he also learns to take her as an interesting, touching, dangerous eccentric like himself, whom he, after their weird marriage (she wounds him with a barbecue fork on their wedding night), can resolve both to "defeat" and to learn to live with, maybe even love.

*Last Notes from Home* is funny, moment by moment, but

it's clearly not the kind of book that *A Fan's Notes* and *Pages from a Cold Island* aspired to be. In them the recognizable details of life (or "life") had to compete with the powers of storytelling to revise life and make it work better; but now storytelling seems to have won out and life to have largely gone elsewhere. The dust jacket of the new book calls it, not a "fictional memoir" (the subtitle of *A Fan's Notes*) but simply "a novel," and that does seem to be all it is. Ex's adventures in Hawaii and the people involved in them sound like entertaining fantasy, something rather desperately cooked up to keep things going. The frisson of embarrassed hope that some of it really happened is missing.

What does survive is Ex's voice, now somewhat more fluent and surer of its effects but still expressive of the role he's played all along. That role is familiar in its general contours but enough different from its literary antecedents—in Henry Miller, Mailer, Thurber, Hemingway, Céline, and others—to be interesting in its own right. The American macho man is well enough known; the bars, as I've said, are full of them, in the pink or sinking fast, pouring out their tales of prowess, real or imagined. Ex is made of such stuff, with his deplorable views of women, his suspicions of blacks and Asians, his readiness for physical and verbal violence, his love of heroic images even while assuming that in real life "great" people are mostly crooks or phonies. But he endearingly doesn't quite fit this role, much as he wants to. He's also thoughtful, literary, sensitive inside—born ten or twenty years later he might well have been a hippie, a draft resister, a radical revolutionist. But Ex is too old for social justice; he hasn't an ideological leg to stand on; he couldn't care less about what we're supposed to feel about this and that. He is, I guess, just a recalcitrant, unaccommodated American man, wanting more than there is or ever was to be had. His is not a common type these days, and it's good to hear from him again.

# Index

Acton, John Dalberg, 1st Baron, 113
Adams, Henry, 170, 177–179
Adler, Stella, 126
Agnew, Spiro T., 45, 46, 53
Aldrin, Col. Edwin, 64
Amin, Idi, 207
Anderson, Sherwood, 150
Anger, Kenneth, 62
Angleton, James, 119
Arendt, Hannah, 119
Arlen, Michael J., 124, 125, 131–135
Armstrong, Col. Neil, 64
Austen, Jane, xii, 19

Bach, J. S., 110
Barth, John, xi, 20
Barthelme, Donald, 204
Beach Boys, The, 61
Beatles, The, 13, 35, 59, 77
Beausoleil, Robert, 62
Beck, Julian, 127
Bednarik, Chuck, 234
Beerbohm, Max, 109
Beethoven, Ludwig van, 189
Benny, Jack, 103
Berger, Thomas, xi, 20
Bergstein, Eleanor, 68, 75–78

Bernstein, Leonard, 39, 41–42
Berra, Yogi, 48
Blake, William, 101, 168, 189
Boswell, James, 4
Bouton, Jim, 46, 47–48, 52, 53
Bowne, Walter, 156
Brady, Mathew, 183
Brando, Marlon, 237
Breslin, Jimmy, 229
Brewster, Kingman, 125
Brown, Norman O., 68
Brustein, Robert, 124–131
Buchan, John, 107
Burgess, Anthony, 163
Burroughs, William, 13

Cagney, James, 62
Calley, Lt. William, 52, 64
Calvin, John, 83
"Carlos" (terrorist), 111–112, 119, 195
Carpenter, Edmund, 8
Carrillo, Leo, 62
Carter, Jimmy, 135
Castro, Fidel, 9, 114
Céline, Louis-Ferdinand, 218, 240
Cellini, Benvenuto, 30
Cézanne, Paul, 50, 122

Chandler, Raymond, 80–81, 82, 83
Chekhov, Anton, 74
Chesterfield, Philip Stanhope, 4th Earl of, 30
Clark, Ramsey, 182
Cohen, Leonard, 20
Coles, Robert, 158
Collins, Joan, 211
Columbus, Christopher, x
Condon, Richard, 113–115
Conrad, Joseph, 87, 163
Cooper, Gary, 63
Cooper, James Fenimore, 19, 168
Coover, Robert, 51, 90, 99–105, 107, 205
Cox, Don, 41–42
Crosetti, Frank, 48

Dana, Bill, 114
Dante Alighieri, 14, 134, 147
Darwin, Charles, 164
Davis, Peter, 148–155, 158–161
Day, Doris, 63
Dean, Dizzy, 48
de Lillo, Don, xi
DeMott, Benjamin, 11
Deterding, Sir Henri, 109
Dickens, Charles, 15, 186, 203, 210, 221–222
Dickinson, Emily, 203
Didion, Joan, 170–179
Doctorow, E. L., 99, 107
Dohrn, Bernadine, 43
Douglas, Stephen A., 186
Draper, Ruth, 8
Dulles, Allen and John Foster, 108, 237
Dunne, John Gregory, 192, 214–219
Duston, Hannah, 19, 20

Eden, Anthony, 109
Edison, Thomas Alva, 168
Edwards, Jonathan, 187
Eisenhower, Dwight D., 102–103, 217
Eliot, George, 79
Eliot, T. S., 2, 13, 19, 185
Elkin, Stanley, xi
Elliott, George P., 1
Emerson, Ralph Waldo, ix, xi, xii, 228
Empson, William, 48
Epstein, Edward Jay, 108–111
Epstein, Jason, 93
Erdman, Paul, 111
Exley, Frederick, 51, 230–240

Falwell, Jerry, 188, 205
Fanon, Frantz, 2
Farrakhan, Louis, 188
Faulkner, William, xi, 203
Ferber, Edna, 239
Fiedler, Leslie, 16–23, 24
Field, Sally, 211
Finch, Peter, 135
Fitzgerald, F. Scott, 167, 223
Fleming, Ian, 109, 110
Forster, E. M., 163
Franklin, Benjamin, 168
Freud, Sigmund, 117
Frost, Robert, xi
Fugs, The, 3
Fuller, Buckminster, 168

Gazzara, Ben, 237
Giamatti, A. Bartlett, 130
Gifford, Frank, 233–234, 237
Ginsberg, Allen, 31
Goldman, Eric, 6
Graham, Billy, 182
Grant, U. S., 102
Grass, Günter, 31

# Index

Graves, Robert, 68
Greene, Graham, 163
Griffin, Merv, 135
Gulbenkian, Calouste and Nubar, 108, 110
Gumble, Bryant, 204
Gutenberg, Johann, 183, 185

Hamilton, Alexander, 186
Hammett, Dashiell, 80–81, 82, 83
Harlow, Jean, 63
Hart, Gary, 205
Hart, William S., 63
Hawthorne, Nathaniel, 133–134, 168, 232
Hefner, Hugh, 30
Heinlein, Robert, 58
Heisenberg, Werner, 13
Heller, Joseph, xi
Hellman, Lillian, 91, 93–94, 96
Hemingway, Ernest, xi, 210, 240
Henry, Alexander, 19
Herlihy, James Leo, 20
Herman, Babe, 48
Hitler, Adolf, 59, 129
Hobbes, Thomas, 198
Holzer, Baby Jane, 26
Homer, 134, 197–198
Howard, Ken, 127
Huizinga, Johann, 34

Irving, Washington, 19

Jagger, Mick, 186
James, Henry, 19, 79, 87
James, William, 138, 228
Jefferson, Thomas, 30, 102, 185, 186, 228
Johnson, Lyndon B., 64, 77, 100, 236

Jones, Jim, 207
Joyce, James, 2, 11, 14, 67, 145, 185, 210, 239

Keats, John, 234
Kennedy, Edward, 182
Kennedy, Robert, 56–57, 76
Kennedy family, 96, 113
Kenner, Hugh, 11
Kermode, Frank, 1, 5
Kerr, Deborah, 210
Kesey, Ken, 20, 25, 26, 27–29, 32, 35–36, 42, 63
King, Martin Luther, Jr., 239
King, Stephen, 192, 201–207
Kipling, Rudyard, 163
Kissinger, Henry, 64, 109
Koch, Edward, 156
Kramer, Jerry, 51

Larson, Jack Lenor, 41
Laurencin, Marie, 122
Lawrence, D. H., 20, 63–64, 79
Leary, Timothy, 91
Leavis, F. R., 19
le Carré, John, 194
Lehrer, Jim, 189
Leonard, Elmore, 192, 209–214, 218
Lerman, Rhoda, 68–72, 75, 78
Lévi-Strauss, Claude, 2, 23
Lewis, Meriwether, 20
Lewis, Oscar, 158
Lewis, Percy Wyndham, 13, 185
Lincoln, Abraham, 102, 182–183, 186, 188
Lindsay, John V., 49
Locke, John, 183
Lombardi, Vincent, 51
Lovecraft, H. P., 202
Luce, Clare and Henry, 217

Ludlum, Robert, 192–199
Lynd, Helen and Robert, 150

McCarthy, Eugene, 76–77, 122
McCarthy, Joseph P., 93, 95, 100, 110
McCarthy, Mary, 117–123, 171
Macdonald, Dwight, 1, 14
Macdonald, Ross, 80–84, 86, 87, 89
McGovern, George, 236
McLuhan, Marshall, xvi, 1–15, 24, 31, 170, 183–185, 188
McNamara, Robert, 64
MacNeill, Robert, 189
Madison, James, 185
Maglie, Sal, 48
Mailer, Norman, xi, 17, 55, 171, 237, 240
Manson, Charles, 54–65
Mantle, Mickey, 48, 49
Marlowe, Christopher, 17
Marx, Karl, 117
Marx Brothers, 103
Mattei, Enrico, 108
Maugham, W. Somerset, 163
Meggysey, Dave, 45, 46–47, 49, 53
Melville, Herman, 148, 163, 167, 168, 172, 230
Meredith, George, 6
Miller, Henry, 240
Miller, Jonathan, 1, 14
Millet, Kate, 237
Milton, John, 83
Montaigne, Michel de, 18
Morrison, Toni, xi
Morse, Samuel F. B., 184
Moses, Robert, 70
Mossadeq, Mohammed, 108, 111
Mozart, W. A., 50

Murray the K, 26
Murrow, Edward R., 155

Nabokov, Vladimir, 237
Nesbit, E., 202–203
Newman, Paul, 77
Newsom, Bobo, 48
Nixon, Patricia, 102
Nixon, Richard M., 45, 47, 49, 51, 64, 99, 100, 102–104, 182

Oates, Joyce Carol, xi
Oates, Titus, 11
Ong, Walter J., SJ, 11
Oppenheim, E. Phillips, 107
Orwell, George, 95, 163
Oswald, Lee Harvey, 77, 114

Paar, Jack, 13
Pascal, Blaise, 138, 140
Phillips, David Atlee, 111–112
Phillips, William, 49
Picasso, Pablo, 189
Piercy, Marge, 68, 72–75, 78
Plato, 183
Pocahontas, 19
Poe, Edgar Allan, 12, 168
Poirier, Richard, 51, 167
Pope, Alexander, 101
Postman, Neil, 170, 181–191
Pound, Ezra, xi, 13, 185
Pynchon, Thomas, 107, 204

Quayle, Dan, 236
Quinton, Anthony, 5

Raleigh, Sir Walter, 17
Rather, Dan, 189
Raymond, Bugs, 48

# Index

Reagan, Ronald, 135, 148–149, 160, 182, 187–188, 212
Reed, Ishmael, xi, 71–72, 99, 107
Reeves, Richard, 148–149, 155–161
Rembrandt van Rijn, 120
Richardson, Samuel, 67, 79
Ricks, Christopher, 1
Rogers, Will, 62
Rohatyn, Felix, 157
Rohmer, Sax, 107
Rolling Stones, The, 34
Romberg, Sigmund, 111
Roosevelt, Kermit, Jr., 109
Rosenberg, Ethel and Julius, 99, 100, 101, 103–104
Rosenberg, Harold, 1, 11
Rossetti, Dante Gabriel, 30, 108
Roth, Philip, xi
Rousseau, Jean-Jacques, 13

Sanders, Ed, 54, 56–60, 62, 63
Savio, Mario, 32
Schwartzkopf, H. Norman, 108
Scott, Sir Walter, 89
Scott, Willard, 204
Sebring, Jay, 63
Seferis, George, 203
Shah Reza Pahlevi, 109, 118
Shakespeare, William, 18
Shapiro, Karl, 203
Shaw, George Bernard, 15
Sheen, Fulton J., SJ, 217
Sheldon, Sidney, 229
Shepard, Sam, 128–129
Shire, Talia, 127
Shore, Dinah, 135
Sidney, Sir Philip, 123
Siqueiros, David, 112
Sirhan, Sirhan, 57

Smith, Capt. John, 19
Somoza, Anastasio, 211
Sontag, Susan, 1
Spector, Phil, 30
Stalin, Josef, 94, 95, 97
Stearn, G. E., 3, 5, 8
Steinem, Gloria, 237
Steiner, George, 1
Strathalmond, William Fraser, 1st Lord, 109
Streep, Meryl, 127
Sullivan, Ed, 35, 77
Sun Yat-Sen, 107
Swaggart, Jimmy, 187
Swift, Jonathan, 15, 187, 218
Symmes, John Cleves, 152

Taft, William Howard, 182
Tate, Sharon, 54, 59, 60, 62
Taylor, Elizabeth, 76
Teagle, Walter, 109
Terkel, Studs, 158
Theroux, Paul, 81, 84–89, 148, 163–169
Thoreau, Henry David, 20, 22, 163, 228
Thurber, James, 240
Tiepolo, Giovanni Battista, 30
Tocqueville, Alexis de, 148, 155–160, 183
Todd, Mike, 76
Tolkien, J. R. R., 202
Toynbee, Arnold, 13
Trilling, Diana, 90–97
Trilling, Lionel, 93, 96
Trollope, Anthony, 89, 172
Twain, Mark, xi, 19, 163, 187
Twitchell, Karl, 109

Updike, John, 136–147

Van der Weyden, Rogier, 87
Vermeer, Jan, 120, 122
Vidal, Gore, 171
Virgil, 14, 203

Waddell, Rube, 48
Wallace, Edgar, 107
Ward, Artemus, 100
Washington, George, 102
Wawatam, 19
Wayne, John, 64
Weber, Max, 30
Westheimer, Dr. Ruth, 182, 205
Whitman, Walt, xi

Wilkerson, Kathie, 43
Will, George, 221, 228
Williams, William Carlos, xi, 203
Wills, Garry, 93
Wilson, Edmund, 236–237
Winkler, Henry, 127
Wolfe, Tom, 24–43, 220–229
Woolf, Virginia, 72, 79
Wordsworth, William, 205, 207
Wright, Orville and Wilbur, 168

Yastrzemski, Carl, 48
Yeats, W. B., 168